T0333795

AIR CAMPAIGN

THE RUHR 1943

The RAF's brutal fight for Germany's industrial heartland

RICHARD WORRALL | ILLUSTRATED BY GRAHAM TURNER

OSPREY PUBLISHING
Bloomsbury Publishing Plc

Kemp House, Chawley Park, Cumnor Hill, Oxford OX2 9PH, UK
29 Earlsfort Terrace, Dublin 2, Ireland
1385 Broadway, 5th Floor, New York, NY 10018, USA
Email: info@ospreypublishing.com
www.ospreypublishing.com

OSPREY is a trademark of Osprey Publishing Ltd

First published in Great Britain in 2021

A catalogue record for this book is available from the British Library.

ISBN: PB 9781472846563; eBook: 9781472846570;
ePDF: 9781472846549; XML: 9781472846556

22 23 24 25 26   10 9 8 7 6 5 4 3 2

Maps by www.bounford.com
Diagrams by Adam Tooby
3D BEVs by Paul Kime
Index by Alan Rutter
Typeset by PDQ Digital Media Solutions, Bungay, UK
Printed and bound by Bell & Bain Ltd., Glasgow G46 7UQ

To find out more about our authors and books visit www.ospreypublishing.com. Here you will find extracts, author interviews, details of forthcoming events and the option to sign up for our newsletter.

Photo on title page
The attack on Wuppertal-Barmen on 29–30 May, which shows the glow and smoke from incendiaries and a particularly vivid explosion from HE, with its accompanying blast wave. The camera aircraft (from 103 Squadron) and lower-flying bomber are heading northwards, away from the target. (© IWM C 3560)

Author's Acknowledgements
The author would like to express gratitude to the team at Osprey for turning the plain Word documents into this finished product, which has been designed perfectly. Special mention should be made to the Series editor Tom Milner for all his hard work. I must also express thanks to artist Graham Turner, the map designers at Bounford, the BEV (Bird's Eye View) illustrator Paul Kime, and the diagram creator Adam Tooby for their extremely vivid artwork and illustrations which brought the book to 'visual' life. Any errors of fact and detail do, of course, remain the author's responsibility. This book was mainly written throughout the lockdowns of 2020 (tough times for everyone) but many archives continued a remote service, sending documents online. In this regard, sincere thanks go to David Fell of the 103 Squadron Association, Paul Johnson at the National Archives (Kew), Andrew Dennis of the Archives & Library RAF Museum (Hendon), Cristina Neagu at Christ Church Library & Archives (Oxford), the archivist team at Churchill College Archives (Cambridge), the staff at the Imperial War Museum (London) and the Bundesarchiv (Koblenz). Kind permission was given by Pen & Sword for the quotations from the books by Guy Gibson, Arthur Harris and Wilhelm Johnen.

I would like to dedicate this book to Bea, and my parents.

CONTENTS

INTRODUCTION

In the now-famous letter from Arthur Harris to Winston Churchill on 3 November 1943, the Commanding-in-Chief of Bomber Command expressed his wish to 'blitz' Berlin. Doing so with assistance from the US Eighth Air Force, Harris claimed, would win the war. The basis for this claim lay partly on what Bomber Command had already done during 1943. Of the 19 cities in the Ruhr-Rhineland that made up the majority of Bomber Command's target list, Cologne, Essen, Dortmund, Dusseldorf, Bochum, Mulheim, Köln-Deutz, Wuppertal-Barmen/Elberfeld, Mönchengladbach/Rheydt, Krefeld, Aachen and Remscheid were all classified as 'Virtually Destroyed'[1], while Duisburg, Hagen, Münster and Oberhausen were labelled as 'Seriously Damaged', and only Leverkusen was in the merely 'Damaged' category. In addition, with the Ruhr being a largely continuous urban area, it was stated that 'vast "casual" damage in certain built-up areas outside the towns named' had also occurred. Such categorization meant the Ruhr was described as being 'largely "out"' and thus 'much progress', Harris claimed, 'has been made towards the elimination of the remaining essentials of German war power', with the Ruhr over half way towards 'collapse'.

This had been the first stage of Harris' 'Main Offensive' against Germany, which comprised three air campaigns against the Ruhr, Hamburg and Berlin. Bomber Command was sent again and again to the same target in the hope of destroying it completely. Alternative targets sometimes had to be raided, both to keep the German defences guessing and because of weather factors, but the Germans realized what was happening and concentrated their defences at the main target. This resulted in such fierce opposition for the bombers that the conflicts were later classed as 'Battles'.

1   Targeted German cities were classified as either 'Virtually Destroyed', which was defined as 'devastation to a degree which makes the objective a liability to the total German war effort vastly in excess of any assets remaining'; 'Seriously Damaged', which meant a 'percentage destruction greater than anything which we have experienced'; or the final category, simply 'Damaged'.

Several characteristics should be borne in mind about this air campaign: first, the Battle of the Ruhr was the least controversial of the World War II bombing offensives, unlike that against Hamburg, whose fiery destruction provoked both contemporary concern and subsequent condemnation; or the one against Berlin, which proved controversial because of the clear schism between the Air Staff and Harris over bombing strategy at that time. In contrast, there was never controversy over the Ruhr air campaign. The Air Ministry and beyond agreed this area (the industrial engine behind German war production) was entirely 'fair game' for strategic bombing. On the basis of this, the circumstances at the time were far more conducive for Harris continuing this campaign even in the face of mounting losses. Secondly, the wider battle against the Ruhr has traditionally been overshadowed by the famous 'Dambusters' raid, yet Operation *Chastise*, as novel as it was, was only a small part of this much larger story. The Battle of the Ruhr was not only a much bigger operation, but included a number of raids well away from the area. For reasons both of space and to preserve a strict geographical focus on the Ruhr–Rhineland, these raids were not given detailed treatment, except for 'connected' targets, that saw the destruction of arms production at Krupps of Essen followed by strikes on the large Skoda Works at Pilsen, in Nazi-occupied Czechoslovakia.

There were four distinctive air campaigns against the Ruhr-Rhineland industrial area: March–June 1942; March–July 1943; October–November 1944; and March 1945. The last two bombing campaigns against the Ruhr were undertaken when the capabilities of Bomber Command had become truly enormous. The statistics tell their own story: 60,000 tons of bombs were dropped on this region alone in late 1944, whilst March 1945 saw several 1,000-heavy-bomber daylight raids on Essen and Dortmund.

However, the Ruhr campaigns opened with a 1942 battle dogged by technical difficulties. Having taken up his appointment as C-in-C Bomber Command in February 1942, Harris inherited an Air Ministry Directive ordering the resumption of the bomber offensive against Germany. This came after the nadir in Bomber Command's fortunes during the winter of 1941–42, in which its operations had been scaled back substantially to conserve the bomber force prior to the introduction of TR.1335. This device, a radar aid to assist both navigation and bombing known more commonly as 'Gee', was to be used for attacking German cities. 'The primary object of your operations', Harris was told, was 'the morale of the enemy civil population and in particular, of the industrial workers'. The targets were primarily, if not exclusively, the Ruhr cities, not just because they contained a large number of industrial workers but because these lay within Gee's working range (up to 350 miles from RAF Mildenhall). The Directive then set the ambitious goal that 'the cardinal principle which should govern your employment of TR.1335 from the outset should be complete concentration on one target until… its destruction has been achieved'. This stipulation set in motion the concentration of attacks against particular towns, and was, in many ways, the idea behind the later bomber battles of 1943. From February 1942, the primary focus was on four Ruhr cities, starting with Essen, the home of Krupps, then moving onto Duisburg, Düsseldorf, and Cologne, 'first priority targets for the Command', which would be attacked regularly, if unsuccessfully, throughout 1942.

German Minister for Armaments and War Production, Albert Speer. Appointed by Hitler on 8 February 1942, two weeks before Harris became C-in-C Bomber Command, Speer's factories and workers would be the RAF's primary targets during the Battle of the Ruhr. (Getty Images)

The River Rhine c.1930. A natural geographical feature, the Rhine and Ruhr rivers formed a distinctive junction at Duisburg that helped British aircrews ascertain their position over the Ruhr if, of course, weather conditions allowed visual sighting. (Getty Images)

Harris and the 'Bomber Barons' had long argued that strategic bombing was a war-winner, and by the spring of 1943, Bomber Command had built up a large strategic bomber force thanks to British industrial production prioritizing heavy bombers, but at the expense of sending aircraft to RAF Coastal Command and the Mediterranean-Middle East theatre. Harris stated that by doing so, 'we could, during the next year, beyond any shadow of doubt, [then] grind into dust and ashes a sufficiency of the enemy's major cities and resources to make the furthest prosecution of the war impossible to him'. With its aircraft, capabilities and personnel steadily built up over the forthcoming winter, 1943 would be the year in which Bomber Command's results had to fulfil the heady promises given earlier by the 'Bomber Barons'. With Churchill's support, the 'Main Offensive' against Germany, as Harris termed it, thus began in March with the Battle of the Ruhr.

Notwithstanding the destruction caused by certain attacks made during 1942, such as the incendiary raids on Rostock and Lübeck, Bomber Command was, if far from perfect, a much more destructive weapon by 1943. In this regard, the Battle of the Ruhr was a significant milestone in its evolution, as it proved that it could inflict a relatively sustained level of destruction on Germany's industrial cities with increasing consistency. This campaign also taught Bomber Command an awful lot about its own capacities and capabilities, as well as those of its enemy – vital lessons that needed absorbing quickly as Harris' bombing operations went deeper into Germany. This is the story of what was achieved during that landmark air campaign in 1943.

CHRONOLOGY

1942

14 February Sir Arthur Harris Harris appointed C-in-C RAF Bomber Command.

8–9 March to 12–13 April Harris sends Bomber Command eight times to Essen; little damage done owing to inaccurate bombing and the limitations of the bombing device, Gee. The attack on Essen on 10–11 March represents the first operation against Germany by the Avro Lancaster.

30–31 May to 25–26 June Bomber Command launches Thousand-Bomber Raids (Operation *Millennium*) on Cologne, then Essen and finally Bremen. The Mosquito undertakes its first operation to Germany by making a photographic reconnaissance sortie to Cologne on 31 May.

15 August Pathfinder Force formed in 3 Group of the RAF and conducts first operation (against Flensburg) three nights later. Becomes 8 Group in January 1943.

22–23 October to 11–12 December Bomber Command's campaign focuses primarily on bombing northern Italian cities (Turin, Milan and Genoa).

The Pre-Battle Phase

20–21 December Operation: Duisburg (111 Lancasters, 56 Halifaxes, 39 Wellingtons, 26 Stirlings); meanwhile, Oboe bombing system first used operationally against power station at Lutterade (Holland) by six Mosquitoes.

23–24 December to 13–14 January Bomber Command test accuracy of Oboe-led ground-marking techniques on industrial targets in the Ruhr. Starting with small groups of Mosquitoes, they expand to include the Main Force Lancaster Bomber Groups, and comprise 13 trial raids on Essen, Duisburg, Hamborn, Rheinhausen, Meiderich and Düsseldorf.

1943

1 January 6 Group (RCAF) becomes operational.

14–15 January Harris cannot immediately commence the Battle of the Ruhr, owing to the diversion of bombing to other priorities, which includes the U-boat bases in France. That night's attack, against Lorient, marks the start of eight raids against these targets over the forthcoming weeks. Other commitments include bombing Berlin, the German ports of Hamburg and Wilhelmshaven, and Italian targets, which are all attacked during this time.

16–17 January Target-indicators (TIs) first used operationally (Berlin).

21 January Combined Chiefs of Staff issue instruction for the Combined Bombing Offensive (CBO). Amongst other things, it stresses: 'Your primary object will be the progressive destruction and dislocation of the German military, industrial and economic system, and the undermining of the morale of the German people to a point where their capacity for armed resistance is fatally weakened.' Known as the Casablanca Directive, it was issued to Bomber Command (and the US Eighth) on 4 February.

Mk.II Halifaxes taking off in the twilight for another bombing operation. Though not rated by Harris, the Halifax was the unsung hero of RAF Bomber Command and was certainly in the thick of the battle over the Ruhr in 1943. (Tony Buttler Collection)

27–28 January Operation: Düsseldorf (124 Lancasters, 33 Halifaxes, five Mosquitoes); first time Oboe Mosquitoes mark target for Pathfinder Force (PFF) aircraft.

30–31 January Operation: Hamburg (135 Lancasters, six Halifaxes, seven Stirlings); first use of H2S device for target-marking. A frustrating device, Bomber Command would not use it in the forthcoming Ruhr campaign because of Oboe's accuracy, but H2S would be required against long-distance targets during this air campaign, such as bombing Pilsen in Czechoslovakia, which revealed only too clearly the device's drawbacks.

14–15 February Operation: Cologne (90 Halifaxes, 85 Wellingtons, 68 Stirlings); H2S used for dropping sky-markers, which were used when the weather meant the ground could not be seen. Though a troublesome technique when used with H2S, over the Ruhr they could still use Oboe which meant sky-marking had better, if far from perfect, accuracy. Meanwhile, in a dual attack on Germany and Italy, Harris' Lancasters simultaneously made the long trip to bomb Milan.

3 March Molybdenum mine at Knaben attacked by nine Mosquitoes. This material was used for all types of metallurgy, including making alloys. Considerable damage is done in an heroic but largely forgotten low-level daylight raid.

The Battle of the Ruhr

5–6 March Operation (1st): Essen (157 Lancasters, 131 Wellingtons, 94 Halifaxes, 52 Stirlings, eight Mosquitoes). Mosquitoes open the attack by using Oboe, and this operation by 442 aircraft marks the formal beginning of the Battle of the Ruhr. The air campaign will continue for five months until late July.

6 March Harris sends letter of protest over the numerous 'diversions' and multitude of Directives issued to his Command by the Air Ministry. Having started the Battle of the Ruhr, he clearly wants to have a primary focus on bombing Germany reflected in his official bombing instructions.

8–9 March Harris attacks the symbolically Nazi city of Nuremberg, and Munich the following night. Such attacks were undertaken to stretch Germany's air-defences away from the Ruhr. Other non-Ruhr targets attacked during the Battle of the Ruhr were Frankfurt, Stuttgart, Mannheim and Stettin.

10–11 March Bomber Command mounts minor operations during this night; two Mosquitoes from 2 Group bomb Essen and Mülheim, whilst 35 heavy bombers commence minelaying operations along the German coast. These smaller or supporting raids are an often-forgotten aspect of Bomber Command's major air battles.

12–13 March Operation (2nd): Essen (158 Wellingtons, 156 Lancasters, 91 Halifaxes, 42 Stirlings, ten Mosquitoes).

23 March 617 Squadron 'Dambusters' formed at RAF Scampton.

26–27 March Operation (3rd): Duisburg (173 Wellingtons, 157 Lancasters, 114 Halifaxes, nine Mosquitoes, two Stirlings). The first Oboe Mosquito is lost during this attack.

28 March Daylight Operation: Rotterdam Docks (24 Venturas). This effort by 2 Group is undertaken to interfere with the transportation of raw materials down the rivers Waal and Rhine to the Ruhr. A repeat attack would be carried out the following day.

29–30 March Operation (4th): Bochum (149 Wellingtons, eight Mosquitoes). This force suffers high losses of 12 Wellingtons (8.0 per cent); meanwhile, the main heavy-bomber force is sent to attack Berlin.

German night fighter pilots pensively wait for information about an incoming British bomber force. (Getty Images)

2 April First flight by a Mosquito of 1409 (Meteorological) Flight. This important unit allowed Bomber Command to have more up-to-date weather forecast information.

3–4 April Operation (5th): Essen (225 Lancasters, 113 Halifaxes, one Mosquito).

4–5 April Bomber Command sends 577 aircraft to bomb Kiel, a vital destination in the shipment from Scandinavia of raw materials needed by the Ruhr's war industries.

8–9 April Operation (6th): Duisburg (156 Lancasters, 97 Wellingtons, 73 Halifaxes, 56 Stirlings, ten Mosquitoes).

9–10 April Operation (7th): Duisburg (104 Lancasters, five Mosquitoes).

16–17 April Owing to the destruction of Krupps in Essen, Bomber Command attack another major centre of German war production, the Skoda Works in Pilsen, in a very long-range attack. The operation will be repeated on 13–14 May, but owing to H2S's limitations both are failures.

26–27 April Operation (8th): Duisburg (215 Lancasters, 135 Wellingtons, 119 Halifaxes, 78 Stirlings, 14 Mosquitoes).

28–29 April Bomber Command undertakes a large minelaying operation (comprising 207 aircraft) in the sea-lanes to Germany's ports around Heligoland and the Danish Belts, and also in the Elbe's estuary. It proves a costly attack, with 22 aircraft (10.6 per cent) being lost.

30 April–1 May Operation (9th): Essen (190 Lancasters, 105 Halifaxes, ten Mosquitoes).

4–5 May Operation (10th): Dortmund (255 Lancasters, 141 Halifaxes, 110 Wellingtons, 80 Stirlings, ten Mosquitoes).

12–13 May Operation (11th): Duisburg (238 Lancasters, 142 Halifaxes, 112 Wellingtons, 70 Stirlings, ten Mosquitoes).

13 May After many failures and uncertainties, a successful explosion test of Upkeep 'bouncing bomb' is achieved.

13–14 May Operation (12th): Bochum (135 Halifaxes, 104 Wellingtons, 98 Lancasters, 95 Stirlings, ten Mosquitoes). The Lancasters make the long-distance trip once again to Pilsen.

16–17 May Operation (13th): Ruhr Dams (19 Lancasters). This famous attack sees the Möhne and Eder dams breached, but the Sorpe and Schwelme dams remain standing. Eight aircraft (42 per cent) fail to return.

23–24 May Operation (14th): Dortmund (343 Lancasters, 199 Halifaxes, 151 Wellingtons, 120 Stirlings, 13 Mosquitoes). With a total of 826 aircraft dispatched, this is the largest attack of the Battle of the Ruhr, and causes considerable damage.

25–26 May Operation (15th): Düsseldorf (323 Lancasters, 169 Halifaxes, 142 Wellingtons, 113 Stirlings, 12 Mosquitoes). Unlike the previous night's operation, this attack is a considerable failure.

27 May 14 Mosquitoes from 105 and 109 Squadrons make the long trip in daylight to bomb factories at Jena at low level (the factories make components for the Würzburg radars and plotting tables for the Kammhuber Line night air defence system). The squadrons are then transferred from 2 Group to the PFF.

27–28 May Operation (16th): Essen (274 Lancasters, 151 Halifaxes, 81 Wellingtons, 12 Mosquitoes).

29–30 May Operation (17th): Wuppertal-Barmen (292 Lancasters, 185 Halifaxes, 118 Stirlings, 113 Wellingtons, 11 Mosquitoes). The attack is devastating, probably the most destructive of the entire battle, and sees a 'firestorm' (most associated with Hamburg) develop.

10 June Pointblank Directive issued. This reiterates the general aim of the Casablanca Directive, but adds ball-bearing plants and Germany's aircraft industries as a priority.

16 June Responding to a query from Air Chief Marshal Charles Portal, Chief of the Air Staff, Harris explains his thinking on future bombing strategy. 'We will then go progressively further into Germany in I hope sufficient strength to be able to leave behind us, as we progress, a state of devastation similar to that now obtaining in the Ruhr; if the Boche waits for it,' he writes. From this time, Bomber Command would concentrate on the smaller Ruhr towns, and the cities of the wider Rhineland–Westphalia area.

11–12 June Operation (18th): Düsseldorf (326 Lancasters, 202 Halifaxes, 143 Wellingtons, 99 Stirlings, 13 Mosquitoes) and Münster (29 Lancasters, 22 Halifaxes, 21 Stirlings). The latter attack is undertaken solely by 8 Group's heavy bombers, which all use H2S.

12–13 June Operation (19th): Bochum (323 Lancasters, 167 Halifaxes, 11 Mosquitoes).

14–15 June Operation (20th): Oberhausen (197 Lancasters, six Mosquitoes).

16–17 June Operation (21st): Cologne (202 Lancasters, ten Halifaxes). Like the earlier attack on Münster, the PFF use H2S for target-marking, rather than Oboe.

20–21 June Bomber Command undertake Operation *Bellicose*, which involves bombing the Zeppelin Works at Friedrichshafen on the Swiss–German border, before going on to land in North Africa. This factory produced the Würzburg radars that were an essential element of the Kammhuber Line, which Bomber Command had to penetrate in order to attack targets in the Ruhr–Rhineland area.

21–22 June Operation (22nd): Krefeld (262 Lancasters, 209 Halifaxes, 117 Stirlings, 105 Wellingtons, 12 Mosquitoes).

22–23 June Operation (23rd): Mülheim (242 Lancasters, 155 Halifaxes, 93 Stirlings, 55 Wellingtons, 12 Mosquitoes). Following losses of 44 aircraft (6.2 per cent) the previous night, Bomber Command sustains 35 heavy bombers missing (6.3 per cent) on this operation, 34 aircraft (5.4 per cent) on the next Ruhr operation and 13 aircraft (6.4 per cent) on 25–26 June. Such losses (126 aircraft in total) in four operations over five nights show that the Battle of the Ruhr is becoming increasingly costly.

24–25 June Operation (24th): Wuppertal-Elberfeld (251 Lancasters, 171 Halifaxes, 101 Wellingtons, 98 Stirlings, nine Mosquitoes).

25–26 June Operation (25th): Gelsenkirchen (214 Lancasters, 134 Halifaxes, 73 Stirlings, 40 Wellingtons, 12 Mosquitoes). The target also includes two synthetic-oil plants, but bombing accuracy is poor and results in a costly failure.

28–29 June Operation (26th): Cologne (267 Lancasters, 169 Halifaxes, 85 Wellingtons, 75 Stirlings, 12 Mosquitoes).

3–4 July Operation (27th): Cologne (293 Lancasters, 182 Halifaxes, 89 Wellingtons, 76 Stirlings, 13 Mosquitoes).

8–9 July Operation (28th): Cologne (282 Lancasters, six Mosquitoes).

9–10 July Operation (29th): Gelsenkirchen (218 Lancasters, 190 Halifaxes, ten Mosquitoes).

13–14 July Operation (30th): Aachen (214 Halifaxes, 76 Wellingtons, 55 Stirlings, 18 Lancasters, 11 Mosquitoes).

24–25 July Bomber Command commences battle of Hamburg. Lasting ten days, it comprises four major attacks by the British bombing force including the infamous 'firestorm raid' of 27–28 July. This marks an obvious shift in focus away from the Ruhr.

25–26 July Operation (31st): Essen (294 Lancasters, 221 Halifaxes, 104 Stirlings, 67 Wellingtons, 19 Mosquitoes). One 83 Squadron Lancaster carries the commanding-general of the US Eighth, Brigadier-General Fred Anderson, as an observer. Comprising 705 aircraft, this is a heavy attack that causes considerable devastation to the Krupp Works. The total number of aircraft, and the figures for each type, are considerably more than the bomber force which had attacked this target on 5–6 March at the beginning of the Battle of the Ruhr. This number, together with the replacements needed to cover the huge losses incurred in between, is testimony to the output of Britain's increasingly efficient aircraft factories.

30–31 July Operation (32nd): Remscheid (95 Halifaxes, 87 Stirlings, 82 Lancasters, nine Mosquitoes). This attack represents the Battle of the Ruhr's end, and over the forthcoming weeks Bomber Command shifts its attention to Italy, Peenemünde and Berlin.

Ruhr–Rhineland operations August–November 1943

22–23 August Operation: Leverkusen (257 Lancasters, 192 Halifaxes, 13 Mosquitoes). This attack is designed to hit the important chemical works of IG Farben.

30–31 August Operation: Mönchengladbach-Rheydt (297 Lancasters, 185 Halifaxes, 107 Stirlings, 57 Wellingtons).

14–15 September Operation: Dortmund-Ems Canal. Eight Lancasters of 617 Squadron undertake low-level attack on the embankments of this waterway. Weather forces the recall of aircraft, but the attack is tried again the following night, proving a costly failure. The canal embankments are covered in mist, and five aircraft (63 per cent) are lost.

29–30 September Operation: Bochum (213 Lancasters, 130 Halifaxes, nine Mosquitoes).

1–2 October Operation: Hagen (243 Lancasters, eight Mosquitoes).

3 November Harris sends Churchill a memorandum on the bombing war, and the need for Bomber Command and the USAAF to now attack Berlin to 'cost Germany the war'. (In)famously, he writes: 'I feel certain that Germany must collapse before this programme which is more than half completed already, has proceeded much further. We have not got far to go…' Supporting this view, Harris claims the Ruhr is now 'largely "out"', requiring only occasional 'tidying up all around'. The area is now relegated to the ninth – and last – of the geographically grouped priorities.

3–4 November Operation: Düsseldorf (344 Lancasters, 233 Halifaxes, 12 Mosquitoes) and Cologne (52 Lancasters, ten Mosquitoes). Mk II Lancasters from 3 and 6 Groups use the G-H blind-bombing device to attempt a pinpoint attack on the Mannesmann Steel Works located in Düsseldorf's northern suburbs.

19–20 November Operation: Leverkusen (170 Halifaxes, 86 Stirlings, ten Mosquitoes). A repeat attack against this target proves a considerable failure.

ATTACKER'S CAPABILITIES
Preparing for the 'Main Offensive'

Navigation aids

Before March 1943, the Ruhr had often been a place of expensive disappointment for Bomber Command. Back in late 1940, it was already the subject of suspicion and investigation over whether the targets had been hit as accurately as the aircrews claimed. In particular, an attack on the Krupp Works on 7–8 November by a mixed force of Hampdens, Blenheims and Wellingtons saw HQ Bomber Command find it peculiar that whilst Wellington aircrews observed tremendous fires, the others reported few, all of which pointed to considerable navigational differences.

By spring 1943, Harris wrote that 'at long last we were ready and equipped … [and] at last able to undertake with real hope of success the task which had been given to me when I first took over the Command a little more than a year before, the task of destroying the main cities of the Ruhr'. The key technical development was Oboe, which, combined with new target-marking techniques, would allow Bomber Command to inflict serious damage on the Ruhr. Around since late 1940 and based on the Luftwaffe's Lorenz beams, it was developed by the scientific boffins at the Telecommunications Research Establishment (TRE). With 109 Squadron tasked with assisting its development, a tentative Oboe system had been created by December 1941, and although reliability was initially an issue, Bomber Command was sufficiently impressed to give full support to Oboe's development through 1942. By December, Oboe Mk I was finally ready (Mk II came in October 1943) and operational trials against Ruhr targets were undertaken in early 1943, after which Oboe's accuracy was estimated at 650 yards. Although only one aircraft at a time could be controlled by a pair of Oboe ground-stations over a ten-minute period, from this weakness stemmed the idea of using Oboe to control the target-marking aircraft throughout the duration of the attack. The Oboe ground-marking technique proved relatively straightforward, with only one Mosquito's TIs (Target Indicators) being seen by the 'backers-up' who dropped their markers on this single set of target-markers, but initially this did cause marking problems. As the *British Official History* (the *British Official History on the Strategic Air Offensive against Germany*) states:

The machine which made it possible: the De Havilland Mosquito. The capabilities of the 'Wooden Wonder' in speed and altitude allowed Oboe to operate over the Ruhr with greater accuracy of target-marking. (Tony Buttler Collection)

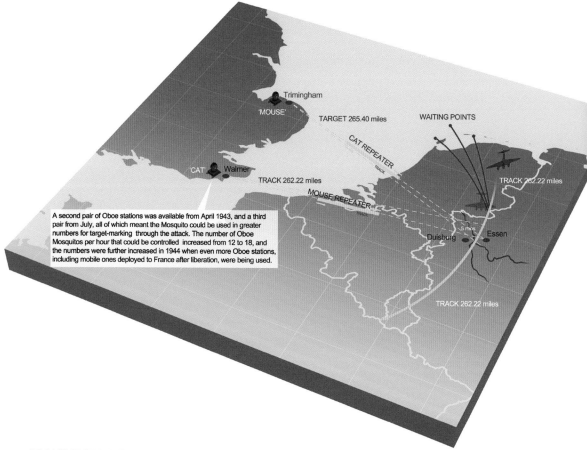

Trimingham
'MOUSE'

TARGET 265.40 miles

WAITING POINTS

CAT REPEATER

'CAT' Walmer

TRACK 262.22 miles

TRACK

TRACK 262.22 miles

MOUSE REPEATER

TRACK

5 mns

Duisburg   Essen

A second pair of Oboe stations was available from April 1943, and a third pair from July, all of which meant the Mosquito could be used in greater numbers for target-marking through the attack. The number of Oboe Mosquitos per hour that could be controlled increased from 12 to 18, and the numbers were further increased in 1944 when even more Oboe stations, including mobile ones deployed to France after liberation, were being used.

TRACK 262.22 miles

ABOVE OBOE RADIO BOMBING SYSTEM – THE GAME-CHANGER

First tried out against the power station at Lutterade (in Holland) on 20–21 December 1942 (whilst the Main Force bombed Duisburg), Oboe was used three nights later by five Mosquitoes from 109 Squadron against its first German targets, namely Essen and parts of the sprawling conurbation of Duisburg at Hamborn (northern Duisburg), Meiderich/Beeck (central Duisburg) and Rheinhausen (on the western bank of the Rhine). The development of this instrument would be critical for Harris' ability to attack the Ruhr area both reasonably accurately and in poor weather, as Oboe was a blind-bombing device that guided the aircraft by pulses emitted by two ground-stations in eastern England.

The key to Oboe's operation, noted Professor R. V. Jones, who investigated the workings of the Kammhuber Line, was that 'each aircraft flew on a constant radius from one Oboe station at Trimingham and the correct instant for bomb release was decided by a controller at a second station at Walmer'. As the *British Official History* explains, 'One station, known as the 'Cat', was responsible for the track of the aircraft over the target and the other, known as the 'Mouse', calculated the point on that track at which the bombs should be released. The method of achieving this was to describe an arc through the target of constant range from the 'Cat' station. This arc was, in effect, part of a circle whose circumference passed through the target and whose centre was the 'Cat'. The task of the 'Cat' was to keep the aircraft flying along the arc or, in other words, to keep it moving at a constant distance from itself. This was done by measuring its range and transmitting dots or dashes to indicate deviations to either side of the required track (it seemed to some that the sounds produced by an experimental version of this equipment resembled those emitted by an oboe. Hence arose the code name Oboe). Meanwhile, the 'Mouse' station, which was normally situated about a hundred miles from the 'Cat', was, also by the process of range measurement, able to compute the movement of the aircraft as a component of its progress along a line joining the 'Mouse' station and the target (though the aircraft did not, of course, actually travel along this line). By considering these data and taking into account the ballistics of the bomb or marker to be dropped, the moment to release the weapon could be calculated and signalled to the aircraft.'

For a better reading, the intersection of the two beams was best nearer 90 degrees (30 degrees was considered the minimum). Thus, it becomes clear that the operation of Oboe was never weather dependent, for the system did not rely on visual identification of the target, and so was perfect for blind-bombing in cloudy conditions or in the industrial haze often seen hanging over the Ruhr.

Since an Oboe run normally took about ten minutes this meant that only six Oboe-directed bombs or markers could be dropped in the space of an hour. Target indicators generally burned for only six minutes, which meant that Oboe marking was, in the early stages, certain to be punctuated with four-minute gaps, and in the event of a single Oboe run failing, the gap would be extended to fourteen minutes.

Although this was less of a problem if earlier bombing had caused significant fires to take hold around the aiming-point before the TIs went out, the onus was very much on the Main Force to maintain navigational discipline and adhere to a strict bombing timetable. Opening more Oboe stations, and also operating aircraft on multiple frequencies, would help to lessen this problem, but such solutions would not be available for the Battle of the Ruhr's early stages. Nonetheless, poor weather over the Ruhr was no longer the monumental barrier to accurate bombing attacks it once had been, and R. V. Jones later wrote, 'as it turned out, Oboe was the most precise bombing system of the whole war'.

Like Gee, Oboe was susceptible to German jamming and, though hindered by its lack of range – at 20,000ft, Oboe's range was about 200 miles – the higher-flying Mosquito could achieve 270 miles when flying at 28,000ft. Aircraft flying higher increased Oboe's range owing to the curvature of the earth, and it was for this reason that the Mosquito, with its much greater ceiling, was especially favoured. The Mosquito's speed also made it less susceptible to German defences while making the Oboe run to the target, and thereby lessened the chance of violent evasive action. Notwithstanding the range limitation, all of the Ruhr could be attacked using Oboe; however operating further afield plunged Bomber Command into the uncertain world of H2S's performance. To free aircraft from a technical device's range restriction and German jamming, Bomber Command saw the need for a device carried in the aircraft itself. Also tested operationally in early 1943, H2S is important to mention given that Harris' strategy during the Battle of the Ruhr was to also attack targets well away from the primary target area. This was both tactical – to spread Germany's air defences over a wide area – and intentional, for fulfilling the overriding aim of the Casablanca Directive meant destroying all German war industries, not just those located in the Ruhr–Rhineland. Thus, following the heavy attacks on the Krupp Works in Essen, it seemed logical to bomb the giant Skoda Works at Pilsen, which was attempted twice, although on both occasions H2S caused inaccurate bombing.

H2S and Oboe would undergo continual development work in a quest for better consistency and accuracy. But in March 1943, as Webster and Frankland conclude, although these devices 'had their limitations and disadvantages and some were double-edged weapons … their introduction had a revolutionary effect upon the ability of Bomber Command to find and hit its targets'. Yet the Oboe Mosquito, a vital weapon in the conduct of the Ruhr campaign remained in short supply, whilst one-in-three aircraft suffered equipment failure upon reaching its target. Given the limitation of the number of ground-stations available during the early part of the battle, Oboe's malfunctioning was a serious drawback as a maximum of 12 Oboe Mosquitoes could be controlled over a target within a 60-minute period. Almost inevitably, 'we were never able to maintain absolute continuity of marking' during the early Ruhr operations, Harris wrote, although things did improve when a third pair of Oboe ground-stations became operable and were used on the Essen operation of 25–26 July.

Aircraft

Beyond technical aids, the other notable feature was Bomber Command's composition and expansion prior to the Battle of the Ruhr. In many ways the aircraft that permitted the Battle of the Ruhr to be undertaken was the de Havilland Mosquito. Famously made entirely from wood, which meant construction was much less complex than metal-framed aircraft, nearly

An impressive view of a Mk.III Wellington. Considered a medium bomber, the Wellington continued to be used extensively on German operation until autumn 1943. This particular aircraft, X3763 (KW-E), belonged to 425 (RCAF) Squadron and would be shot down by a Bf 110 of IV/NJG-4 over France on the Stuttgart operations of 14–15 April. (Tony Buttler Collection)

7,800 were produced; an impressive number given its initial rejection by the Air Ministry. A private project of de Havilland, it was designed and tested in record time. Fast and high-flying, the Luftwaffe's night fighters – often weighed down by equipment and antennas – rarely saw them, let alone shot them down, despite the Mosquito having to fly straight and level for a prolonged period to allow Oboe to assist with accurate marking of the target. From 485 sorties flown during the Ruhr campaign,[2] only four Mosquitoes were lost and another six returned damaged. Though able to conduct low-level attacks, such as that against the molybdenum mines at Knaben on 3 March 1943, the Battle of the Ruhr saw the Mosquito's high-flying capabilities allowed for the full exploitation of Oboe over the Ruhr and, hence, its primary target-marking role. It was, the *British Official History*, concludes, 'the hinge upon which the whole tactical plan for the attack on the Ruhr turned'. Without the Mosquito, Oboe's restrictions would have likely led to disappointing results that mirrored the Gee-led campaign against the Ruhr of the previous year.

The Oboe-equipped Mosquitoes of the PFF thus proved the final ingredient for commencing the Battle of the Ruhr. Oboe Mosquitoes possessed a non-transparent nose, with the normal glass area – usually reserved for the bomb-aimer – painted over and the compartment being utilized for the Oboe equipment. As well as target-marking duties, Oboe-equipped Mosquitoes were used for bombing specific targets, such as the Krupp Works or the Gelsenkirchen-Nordstern synthetic-oil plant, which 105 Squadron attacked on 9–10 July. No. 8 Group had inherited this squadron from 2 Group in April 1943, from which its Oboe capability developed, and it was soon expanded to three flights. Air Vice-Marshal Donald Bennett also had 139 Squadron, which he used as a 'supporter squadron' for the early target markers, for undertaking diversionary attacks 'to attract fighters away from the mainstream at appropriate moments during the attack', and for 'nuisance' attacks in which batches of Mosquitoes (ranging from four to30 aircraft) would attack a German city to set off the air-raid sirens, thereby straining civilian morale and interrupting war production. Able to carry a 4,000lb blockbuster bomb (or 'cookie'), they were sometimes sent to another part of the Ruhr–Rhineland area, while 'nuisance' raids to Berlin were also undertaken. Mosquitoes were also used for another crucial role, the missions of 1409 Met Flight. Based at RAF Oakington and commencing operations on 2 April, this flight was charged with obtaining the latest weather information. Vital considerations such as the extent of cloud cover and wind-speed and its direction, both along the routes and over the target, was needed before HQ Bomber Command took its final operational decisions on operations.

By May 1943, the PFF had expanded considerably, not just because of its added Mosquito components from 2 Group but also through the addition of new four-engined units transferred from the Main Force, with 97 (Straits Settlement) Squadron and 405 (Vancouver) Squadron arriving from 5 Group and 6 Group respectively. All this reflected an overall expansion of Bomber Command by March 1943. In the major attack on Duisburg on 20–21 December 1942, for example, Harris had sent 232 aircraft – a number that was a consequence of a 'slack' period of operations and the low losses incurred on the series

2   Be they independent attacks on heavily defended places such as Berlin and Munich, or target-marking operations flown by the PFF.

of Italian raids over the previous months. Though this was certainly better than the force Harris had inherited, which had comprised only four Bomber Groups of Wellingtons and the increasingly obsolete Whitleys, Hampdens and Manchesters, the number of aircraft continued to worry Harris throughout 1942. In early December that year, Harris spoke of being 'disturbed at the deterioration in the Heavy and Medium position for November as compared with October' owing to sluggish production of all types, especially the Stirling, in which Bomber Command would end November with five less than it had at the beginning. As for his entire force, he told Portal on 25 December that:

> On January 1st we shall be down five squadrons on the expansion programme, have lost the equivalent of six squadrons to Torch and had practically the whole operational value of 3 Group collapse under us owing to the scandalous Stirling developments.

The latter was caused by a deficiency of 82 Stirlings, and poorly made examples ('rogues', as Harris termed them) whose ring-wings drooped, elevators were badly made and tails were twisted, and could barely climb to 10,000ft. Five-days later, Harris wrote that 'the Stirling Group has now virtually collapsed' and made 'no worthwhile contribution to our war effort in return for their overheads'. Its notorious maintenance difficulties caused '[a] reduced operational rate and long periods of complete idleness due to the weather, [and] I am lucky if I can raise 30 Stirlings from 3 Group for one night's work after a week of doing nothing, or 20 the night after'. The Stirling, and the poorly performing Halifax, were, he said, 'major worries' that 'presage disaster unless a solution can be found'. As possible solutions, Harris proposed abandoning production of these types in favour of Lancasters, or, at the very least, substituting the Lancasters held in training units with these aircraft. The first request was only partly sanctioned; some Stirling factories would be switched over to Lancaster production but the five Halifax factories would not follow suit. Headway would be made with the second consideration, with Lancasters soon being replaced in the HCUs (Heavy Conversion Units, designed to train aircrews for operations on four-engine heavy bombers) by the other types. Nonetheless, on 21 January 1943, Air Vice-Marshal Robert Saundby, Senior Air Staff Officer at HQ Bomber Command gave Harris the 'not very cheerful' news that 'no further expansion of heavy squadrons, even by the creation of third flights, is envisaged before 1st April'. In a handwritten comment, Harris noted, 'this is very depressing', but it was this force, far from expanded in number, which he would use for commencing the Ruhr air campaign on 5–6 March.

By mid-1943,however, a proper flow of heavy bombers was in process. Bomber Command thus went from 45 operational heavy and medium bomber squadrons in January 1943 to 50 three months later, whilst each individual squadron on average had increased from 17 to 21 aircraft. Thus, the force of 442 aircraft which had opened the Battle of the Ruhr was, just over two months later, increased substantially when Harris sent 826 bombers to Dortmund on 23–24 May. Bomber Command's

The Short Stirling I. The type's complicated undercarriage and height from the runway can be clearly seen; less obvious was its low ceiling which saw Stirling crews often going over the Ruhr at the lethally low altitudes of between 12,000–14,000ft. Mines appear to be loaded into this aircraft, from 218 (Gold Coast) Squadron, ready for a minelaying sortie. (Tony Buttler Collection)

average strength throughout the Ruhr air campaign was 794 heavy bombers (a substantial part being Lancaster squadrons), in which 578 machines (73 per cent) were serviceable. There was no doubt the British aircraft industry had become properly geared for waging the strategic bombing offensive.

The Command's one reduction was 2 Group, the unit that comprised Boston, Ventura, Mosquito and Mitchell light bombers and which had undertaken some spectacular daylight operations over German-occupied North-West Europe, such as the attack on the Philips Factory in Eindhoven on 6 December 1942. This often-overlooked bomber group would play its part during the Battle of the Ruhr, conducting intruder activity against enemy airfields and bombing precise targets from low level, such as the molybdenum mines at Knaben in Norway, the Rotterdam Docks and Jena's optical instrument factory on 27 May. As brave as these attacks were, 2 Group was becoming a concern owing to its mostly obsolete aircraft that had to operate in daylight. On 1 June 1943, it was transferred to the Second Tactical Air Support to begin army-support training, although its Mosquitoes of 105 and 139 squadrons would be given to the Pathfinders.

The Lancaster's superior capabilities – particularly the Mk I and III variants – in terms of range, ceiling and bombload capacity, are well known, with its ability to carry a heavier bombload higher, farther and faster than the Halifax, Stirling or the American types, the B-17 and B-24. The Lancaster could carry the largest bombs and was selected for modification to carry Barnes Wallis' 'special' bomb for destroying the Ruhr Dams. But the Mk II/V Halifax was, like the Stirling, fast becoming obsolete and frequently struggled to perform. One experienced 4 Group Commander, Group Captain Tom Sawyer, who flew the Halifax Mk II for 51 Squadron during the Battle of the Ruhr, wrote later that the extra equipment and the greater petrol and bombloads all strained the aircraft's engines and reduced the type's operational height to well below that of the Lancaster. This meant greater vulnerability to flak and night fighters, and increased danger of being hit by bombs and incendiaries dropped from higher-flying aircraft, a terror many former aircrew always remembered. Meanwhile, from its numerous serious weaknesses, the Stirling's most significant danger for bombing the Ruhr was also its inability to achieve a higher ceiling for flying over this flak-infested area.

Pathfinders (PFF)

Alongside its technical devices and expanding size, there was a third element that helped Harris conduct the Ruhr air campaign: the Pathfinders. Created during summer 1942, the PFF's first operation was a response to the long-standing problems of both finding and marking the target. Its initial performance was hamstrung by the limitations of its equipment, as much as anything else, and it would be a mistake to think the PFF's creation led to a sudden improvement in results. For the rest of 1942, a greater number of aircraft were bombing nearer the aiming-point, but failures remained, especially attacks made in the poorer weather of autumn 1942 against Flensburg, Frankfurt, Saarbrucken, Cologne and Hamburg – the latter being a particularly dreadful performance – and many months of trial and error lay ahead before a breakthrough was made. At this stage, the PFF illuminated the target using some often ad hoc markers, which included large bombs filled with rubber and phosphorous, to distinguish these from the incendiary bombs dropped by other aircraft. Moreover, the Main Force was instructed to use the PFF's marking only as a guide, and was, in fact, expected to find the aiming-point themselves. It must be stressed that the primary purpose of the Pathfinder Force in 1942, perhaps as the name suggested, was leading the way to the target;

A Mk.II Lancaster of 61 Squadron. This aircraft would be transferred to 115 Squadron and lost on the Frankfurt operation of 10–11 April 1943. The distinctively square engine nacelles, which housed the variant's Bristol Hercules engines, can be clearly seen. (Tony Buttler Collection)

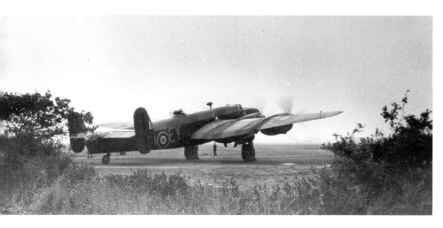

Handley-Page Halifax Mk.II of 78 Squadron ('EY') taking off from RAF Linton-on-Ouse. The bleakness of Bomber Command's airfields can be seen clearly. (Tony Buttler Collection)

it was a specialist force of navigators, not bombers. Yet by spring 1943, the arrival of Oboe, the Mosquito and new marker-bombs (target-indicators, or TIs) had all contributed to the PFF now being an actual target-marking force. In particular, TIs allowed the PFF to mark the aiming-point more prominently, for they ignited not upon ejection but on the ground, with explosive candles designed to discourage German firefighters; overall, a target-indicator of 250lb illuminated an area of about 100 yards. Testimony to the full mobilization of the British firework and chemical industry, bright white TIs would be used for visual ground-marking (known as Newhaven). In cloudy weather, the technique deployed was called blind sky-marking (Wanganui),[3] in which the sky-marker – in effect a TI candle with a parachute, and produced in the three-colours of red, green and yellow to indicate the various stages of the marking process – had to be deployed because ground-markers could simply not been seen. The sky-marker burst with a candelabra effect, which made a Bomber Command attack a colourful if ultimately deadly display of pyrotechnics, but its drawbacks were a short period of burning and, even more seriously, the tendency to drift in the altitude winds, both of which meant they needed constant replacing. Sky-markers were themselves sometimes not always enough; the Düsseldorf operation on 25–26 May saw the thick cloud up to 20,000ft simply swallow them up and render them invisible. After the war, Harris admitted that sky-marker attacks 'did not always go according to plan', and generally they never proved as effective as ground-marking, especially if used in conjunction with H2S. Nonetheless, as imperfect as they were, they did at least allow Bomber Command to continue to operate in poor weather with some reasonable prospect of inflicting worthwhile damage on a target.

Overall, TIs proved, according to the *British Official History*, 'a singularly welcome prospect to anxious and harassed crews who otherwise would have been searching for the aiming-point'. After February 1943, Main Force crews were ordered to drop their bombs on the TIs once seen, rather than dangerously spending time in the busy target area locating the aiming-point for themselves. Of course, the pressure on PFF crews had increased, with any errors likely to mean the entire attack becoming a failure. Yet the great advantage of this new approach was it allowed the bombers to get over and away from the target as quickly as possible, something which HQ Bomber Command certainly believed helped reduce the casualty figure.

Finally, there came the actual means of destroying the target and, during the campaign, Bomber Command would drop a whole array of ordnance: high-explosive bombs (HEs), incendiary bombs (IBs), air-laid mines and special bombs (such as 'Upkeep'). HEs came in the form of the General Purpose (GP), Medium Capacity (MC) and High Capacity (HC)

3   When Oboe was used to undertake either of these methods, the word 'Musical' was added.

The narrowness of the Lancaster's cockpit and fuselage can be seen from this head-on photograph which disguised its huge bomb bay that carried a tonnage of bombs to Germany's industrial cities. (Tony Buttler Collection)

bombs. What distinguished the latter two was a higher charge-weight ratio so their weight was primarily charge and explosive in a relatively thin casing; these largely superseded GP bombs by early 1942. MC bombs came about because the British had long suspected their GP bombs were proving ineffective, but early versions of the MC were also prone to breaking up on impact. A 1,000lb MC was a success, and used from April 1943, but its supply was never adequate. A 4,000lb MC was also produced, coming into service in early 1943, but only the bomb bay of a Lancaster (and a Mosquito) could carry these weapons. With regards to the HC, its thin casing meant its ability to penetrate structures was much less when compared with thicker-cased bombs, but its 'blast value' was much higher owing to 80 per cent of its weight being charge and explosive. HC 'blockbusters' were, as the *British Official History* noted, the 'primary weapons of the area offensive' and these came in the 4,000lb 'cookie' and 8,000lb versions, both of which Bomber Command's Lancasters would drop on the Ruhr. High-explosive bombs were also produced in 'special' form, which in this air campaign was most famously epitomized by Barnes Wallis' 'bouncing bomb' for use on the Ruhr Dams (its only operation) by the specially trained 617 Squadron.

With regards to IBs, the standard British design by spring 1943 was the 4lb bomb, which used either magnesium or, with this in short supply after the adoption of incendiary tactics, Thermite (an aluminium and iron oxide mixture), which produced great heat and burning qualities – the essential ingredient for destroying areas by fire. Dropped from cluster containers that opened during the descent, thus scattering the individual incendiaries, these projectiles were difficult to aim and could often lead to scattered fires. Yet from March 1943, Bomber Command's increasingly large force that was making more concentrated attacks often meant a greater number of fires within a smaller area, which, if not quickly mastered by the German firefighters, usually joined up to form large conflagrations somewhere near the aiming-point.

A British HE bomb, which were dropped in colossal quantities during the Battle of the Ruhr. Note the message having been chalked on it, this bomb was probably dropped on Cologne on 3–4 July. (Getty Images)

A heavier 30lb IB, filled with phosphorous, was tried in an attempt to stop the scattering, but these were never as widely used and the chief IB weapon remained the 4lb bomb. Indeed, despite its shortcomings, Harris recognized that the 4lb IB 'proved throughout the war [to be] the best weapon for destroying large industrial areas'.

One other piece of ordnance dropped by Bomber Command during the Battle of the Ruhr, and throughout the war generally, was the air-laid mine. Developed and supplied by the navy, Bomber Command mines had parachutes to slow them down before impact with the water. The standard load was six 1,500lb mines carried by the Lancaster and Stirling, and four 1,000lb mines in the Halifax.

Counter-measures and tactics

In their post-war assessment of the Luftwaffe, the Air Ministry concluded that the German night fighter force had become 'a real threat' to Bomber Command's operations by winter 1942–43. This meant the battle between the RAF and Luftwaffe in the skies over Germany during the following year became 'an ever-recurring cycle of measure and counter-measure, of development and counter-development of radio and radar instruments and tactics'. Bomber Command thus embarked on a two-stage process to overcome the Kammhuber Line, one being technical and the other tactical. With regards to the former, the devices and counter-measures which Bomber Command utilized during the Battle of the Ruhr were Tinsel/Mandrel, Boozer, Monica and Window. 'Science had now truly come to the aid of the bomber in the dark', as Webster and Frankland observed correctly.

Outfoxing the Kammhuber Line could also be achieved through tactical means. Early on, the German air defences were simply flown around, but this was only successful until the Kammhuber Line was expanded. By spring 1943, it was necessary to fly through a portion of it, and thus the tactic adopted was of 'swamping' the German radars by concentrating the bomber stream tightly. This meant that should German radars detect a British bomber, many more would pass through the air defence 'box' undetected. The problem was that while this worked well enough on the outbound route, it was less successful on the return journey when the bomb-run and navigational differences had caused the bomber stream to become much less bunched.

Bomber Command also used other tactical methods, such as false attacks by Mosquitoes and the 'split-attack'. The latter was used on 29–30 March when the bomber force attacked both Berlin and Bochum, and then on 13–14 May (Pilsen and Bochum), which on both occasions saw targets deliberately chosen that were distant from each other and involved two bomber forces flying in different directions. For all this, however, Bomber Command's losses increased noticeably in June because its clear targeting of the Ruhr had become predictable and the Germans could thus concentrate their defences. The light midsummer nights meant Harris had few targets in other, more distant parts of Germany, such as Stuttgart or Munich. By mid-July, he was resolved to switch his bombers to Hamburg, using, of course, Window, bundles of metallized strips dropped in vast quantities, as its main defence; which was used again on 25–26 July when Harris switched back to the Ruhr. This attack on Essen saw 3.7 per cent losses, and an investigation by the Directorate of Bomber Operations (sent to Portal on 27 July) found this compared very favourably to the average 5.4 per cent loss rate for the previous six attacks on that target. Director of Bomber Operations Air Commodore Sydney Bufton therefore calculated that Window had saved 49 bombers on 25–26 July, although losses for the final raid of the Battle of the Ruhr – against Remscheid on 30–31 July – were 5.5 per cent, showing this was hardly a consistent process.

In conclusion, as noted by Professor Richard Overy, the various technical and tactical developments had made Bomber Command 'an incomparably more formidable weapon than it had been in 1942'. Some of its difficulties, if not completely eradicated, had been partially solved, thanks in no small part to Harris' vigorous leadership of the Command. Ultimately, the planning and technology of Bomber Command had become geared to delivering a simple formula: getting to the target, marking the target and destroying the target. Though far from straightforward, and with each element still carrying its own set of difficulties, Bomber Command's enhanced capabilities can, in microcosm, be seen by comparing the damage inflicted on the two Ruhr–Rhineland cities most attacked in 1942, Cologne and Düsseldorf, and the results from attacks on the same cities during the Battle of the Ruhr.

A Lancaster being loaded up with aerial-dropped mines. These weapons would be used extensively by Bomber Command during the war. During the Battle of the Ruhr, they were dropped extensively in the Baltic to stop raw materials being shipped from Scandinavia reaching the Ruhr's war industries. (Getty Images)

DEFENDER'S CAPABILITIES
The rise, fall and rise of Germany's air defences

A Messerschmitt Bf 110 night-fighter. This type, together with the Ju 88, formed the backbone of the GCI system of the Kammhuber Line. Note the array of radio antennas on the aircraft's nose. (Bundesarchiv, Bild 101I-659-6436-12, Fotograf(in): Grosse, Helmut)

Following the opening attack on Essen on 5–6 March, Goebbels noted in his diary that 'Göring's prestige with the Führer had declined hugely', with even some talk of his dismissal. Following a further attack on Essen a week later, the Reich's Propaganda Minister added:

> The Führer told Göring what he thought without mincing words. It is to be expected that Göring will now do something decisive.

But Göring, seemingly consumed by a post-Stalingrad lethargy, continued to be a largely absent figure during the time of the Battle of the Ruhr, and instead it was other senior officers in the Luftwaffe who had the onerous task of trying to stop the heavy bombing.

Night fighters and the Kammhuber Line

Though plans for a German Air Force had been announced by Hitler and Göring in March 1935, it was not until over five years later that a night fighter division was to be added to the Luftwaffe's inventory. The Luftwaffe was intended for offensive operations; air defence, such as it was, revolved solely around flak and searchlights, particularly as Luftwaffe officers had drawn too-optimistic conclusions from the Spanish Civil War about flak's ability to shoot down aircraft. Consequently, in Essen on 8 August 1939, Göring stated that the Ruhr's flak defences meant no hostile aircraft would ever drop a single bomb on the region.

All this changed, however, on 15–16 May 1940, when Bomber Command undertook its first significant bombing raid on Germany, with 100 aircraft sent to attack a range of industrial and transportation targets in the Ruhr. Caught by surprise, and concerned that such an attack was in no way a 'one-off' but instead heralded the beginning of a strategic bombing campaign, the Germans realized that only a dedicated night fighter force could stop the British night bombers. This was created rapidly. Appointed by Göring on 17 July, General

ABOVE LEFT
The 'father' of the
Luftwaffe's night fighter
force, Major Wolfgang
Falck. (© IWM HU
108206)

ABOVE RIGHT
General Josef Kammhuber,
the architect of Germany's
air-defences in the West.
(Bundesarchiv, Bild 146-
1985-017-36,
Fotograf(in): Hoffmann)

osef Kammhuber took up his position as commander of the Luftwaffe's night fighters and was tasked with forming, organizing and equipping its first unit, the 1st Night Fighter Division, and to lay the foundations for the night fighter arm's expansion. Kammhuber himself had shown impressive ability before the war as head of the Luftwaffe's organizational staff, whilst in the subsequent campaign against the Low Countries he had commanded a bombing unit specializing in blind-flying.

Following tentative experiments and some successes in July and August, particularly by Oberleutnant Werner Streib, the development of a significant German air defence system was sanctioned on 30 September. Combining ability with tremendous energy, Kammhuber soon perceived that the night fighters needed assistance from the ground. The first stage of his new defensive line was a 'searchlight belt' in front of western Germany and the Ruhr. With early-warning radars detecting the British approach, the Luftwaffe's night fighters would congregate around beacons in front of the searchlight belt, ready to intercept a bomber when illuminated. This method, given the modest demands placed on it by the small-scale British attacks at this time, worked well enough but was far from perfect. One night fighter pilot, Wilhelm Johnen, later wrote:

As long as the night-fighter pilot had to rely on a machine being caught in the searchlights and could not find his opponent by his own efforts he was virtually helpless. The morale of the crews, which cruised around at night, unable to interfere while the Britishers broke through en masse perhaps twenty miles away, sank to zero.

Consequently, Kammhuber soon pressed for radars to help with night fighting, not just to assist in early warning. This was done so the Luftwaffe's night fighters could locate the British bombers more precisely and so avoid flying in the wrong area. The Würzburg A ground-radar, despite largely having been seized upon its introduction in autumn 1940 by Flak

OPPOSITE THE KAMMHUBER LINE, 1943

Having remained in the Reichswehr after World War I, General Josef Kammhuber transferred to a still-secret Luftwaffe in October 1934 and held various staff appointments up to September 1939. During the French campaign, Kammhuber commanded a long-range bomber unit, Kampfgeschwader 51, and was shot down and taken prisoner in June 1940. Released under the French armistice, he was swiftly appointed to the newly formed German Night Fighter Division in July 1940. After his air-defence system had been invalidated by Bomber Command's use of Window in July 1943, Kammhuber was replaced by General Joseph Schmid. Nonetheless, Kammhuber continued to hold a number of senior appointments in the Luftwaffe until the end of the war before he was captured by the Allies in June 1945 (post-war, he would hold senior positions within the newly formed West German Air Force). Kammhuber's air-defence system took shape in summer 1940 in response to the British night bombing of German cities. Originally modest, it comprised just a handful of flak guns, searchlights and radars. Proving successful, Kammhuber's system had expanded considerably by 1942, both in depth and scope, and at its maximum extent ran from southern Norway to near Paris. It also comprised double defensive 'boxes' and zones around certain inland German cities. Called the *Raumnachtjagd* (literally, space night hunting), Kammhuber's system was based on 'boxes', each of which had its own radars and ground-control staff who guided an airborne night fighter towards an enemy bomber. Though effective, the system was not perfect as only one night fighter could be ground-controlled at any one time – although it was later modified to encompass the control of three aircraft – and was increasingly susceptible to the British tactic of the concentrated bomber-stream, even before the British used Window to 'fog' the German ground radars. By August 1943, Kammhuber's expensive air-defence system had been all but abandoned, with German night fighters being forced into adopting the ad hoc tactic of *Wilde Sau*.

The key ingredient of the Kammhuber Line was the long-range, early-warning *Freya* radar. (Bundesarchiv, Bild 101II-MW-4980-16, Fotograf(in): Richraht)

Command to assist its searchlights and guns, was given in modest numbers to Kammhuber by the Luftwaffe's Director-General of Signals, General Wolfgang Martini. These radar allowed Kammhuber to establish three specific night fighter areas along the route mos likely to be traversed by the British bombers flying to the Ruhr: from Holland back alon the Rhine, in a line some 55 miles long and 12 miles wide. This was very modest indeed owing to only six Würzburgs and three large searchlights being available, but its advantag was immediately apparent. Whilst a night fighter (one flyin in each zone) waited for information from ground control, master searchlight, acting on the information received from the radar and its associated plotting-room, would shine in th right location, thus causing other searchlights to form a con around the targeted British aircraft. In this way, the metho of *Helle Nachtjagd* (illuminated night fighting) was born, an such zones were established both before the Ruhr and aroun the ports of Bremen and Kiel.

But just as Bomber Command's operations were ofte hampered by poor weather, so Kammhuber also had t surmount meteorological issues, especially the problem of heav cloud. He therefore decided to make interception completel reliant on radar. To do so, he procured the Würzburg-Ries (Giant Würzburg) that could detect at a much greater radiu (some 37 miles) and thereby provide ground controllers wit an earlier idea of a possible target, its location and likely cours Simultaneously, another Würzburg tracked the night fighte and both aircraft were plotted on a specially designed tabl in the control room (called a 'T-hut') of each night fighte zone. Through Belgian Resistance agents, the British receive details on how the 'Seeburg Table' worked, with the bombe and fighter's positions portrayed by coloured light spots – re for the former and blue for the latter – which were projecte

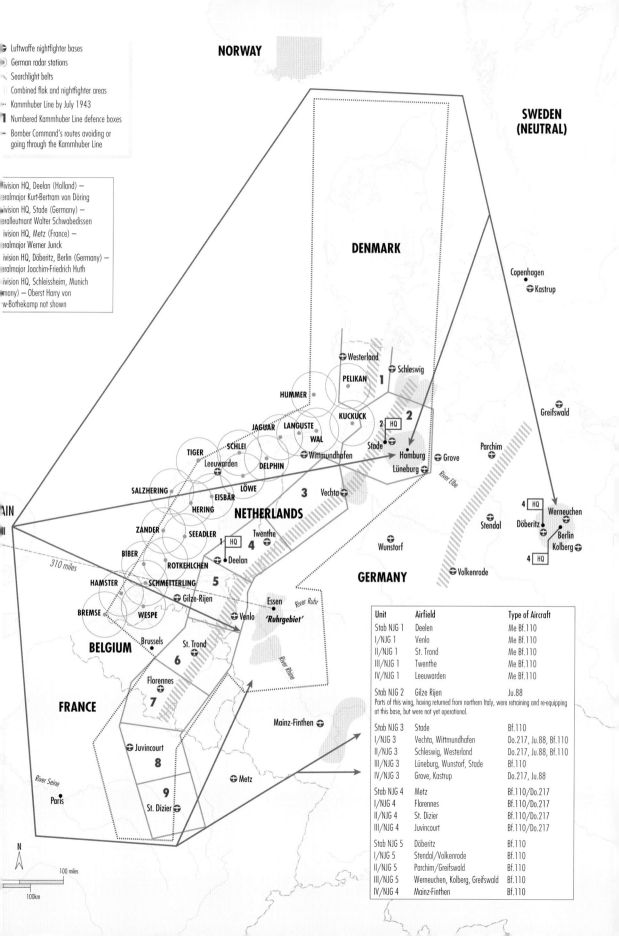

Legend:
- Luftwaffe nightfighter bases
- German radar stations
- Searchlight belts
- Combined flak and nightfighter areas
- Kammhuber Line by July 1943
- **1** Numbered Kammhuber Line defence boxes
- Bomber Command's routes avoiding or going through the Kammhuber Line

...ivision HQ, Deelan (Holland) — ...eralmajor Kurt-Bertram von Döring
...ivision HQ, Stade (Germany) — ...eralleutnant Walter Schwabedissen
...ivision HQ, Metz (France) — ...eralmajor Werner Junck
...ivision HQ, Döberitz, Berlin (Germany) — ...eralmajor Joachim-Friedrich Huth
...ivision HQ, Schleissheim, Munich ...many) — Oberst Harry von ...w-Bothekamp not shown

Unit	Airfield	Type of Aircraft
Stab NJG 1	Deelen	Me Bf.110
I/NJG 1	Venlo	Me Bf.110
II/NJG 1	St. Trond	Me Bf.110
III/NJG 1	Twenthe	Me Bf.110
IV/NJG 1	Leeuwarden	Me Bf.110
Stab NJG 2	Gilze Rijen	Ju.88
Parts of this wing, having returned from northern Italy, were retraining and re-equipping at this base, but were not yet operational.		
Stab NJG 3	Stade	Bf.110
I/NJG 3	Vechta, Wittmundhafen	Do.217, Ju.88, Bf.110
II/NJG 3	Schleswig, Westerland	Do.217, Ju.88, Bf.110
III/NJG 3	Lüneburg, Wunstorf, Stade	Bf.110
IV/NJG 3	Grove, Kastrup	Do.217, Ju.88
Stab NJG 4	Metz	Bf.110/Do.217
I/NJG 4	Florennes	Bf.110/Do.217
II/NJG 4	St. Dizier	Bf.110/Do.217
III/NJG 4	Juvincourt	Bf.110/Do.217
Stab NJG 5	Döberitz	Bf.110
I/NJG 5	Stendal/Volkenrode	Bf.110
II/NJG 5	Parchim/Greifswald	Bf.110
III/NJG 5	Werneuchen, Kolberg, Greifswald	Bf.110
IV/NJG 4	Mainz-Finthen	Bf.110

The other key ingredient of Kammhuber's air defence line was the *Giant Würzburg* radar, which was able to monitor the path of British bomber aircraft. The system, heavily reliant on technology, proved vulnerable to British counter-measures. The 'crisis' of the Kammhuber Line became terminal in late-July 1943. (Getty Images)

from underneath the table on to a large glass screen. The positions of these lights were moved by operators on updated information provided by telephone operators at the Würzburg sites. From this equipment thus developed the method called ground control interception (GCI); the waiting fighter would orbit the zone (or 'box') by using a radio beacon sited within it, before being directed to an interception. The installation of this zonal system, in ever more extensive form, was the final piece in the construction of the Kammhuber Line following the establishment of a dedicated night fighter arm and access to the requisite technology. Eventually comprising many boxes, each with its own radars and ground controllers, the system became increasingly secure because the 'boxes' would come to lie alongside each other, even overlapping, with the main interception chain in front of the Ruhr and thereby designed to prevent British bombers being able to bomb this area by flying directly from the UK. The system provided the Luftwaffe's night fighter crews with two chances to intercept a British attack, for as the AHB's (RAF's Air Historical Branch) post-war study concluded, 'Kammhuber had placed his line of "boxes" in front of the searchlight zones, (and encouraged his night fighter force to attempt interception first under radar control, and if that failed to follow into the searchlight zones.' By early 1941, Kammhuber's air defence system comprised three bands: a coastal belt of Freya early warning radars, the night fighter belt relying on the GCI 'boxes' and the searchlight belt further back towards the Ruhr. Each part communicated with the other. The Kammhuber Line was completed by plotting rooms with properly trained staff and newly created night fighter bases in the Low Countries.

Initially only 150 miles in length in late 1940, throughout 1941 Kammhuber geographically expanded his air-defence system, which by late 1941 saw night fighter 'boxes' (*Raums* to the Germans) running from Denmark all the way to Belgium. This enhanced coverage mean

the Luftwaffe could detect British formations flying towards Germany by a variety of routes, all of which caused Bomber Command to waste precious amounts of fuel to outflank the air defence system by flying further to the north or south. Moreover, as the post-war British Bombing Survey Unit observed:

> The greater the number of boxes crossed by a scattered bomber force, the greater were the opportunities presented to the enemy for engagement. The increasing effectiveness of this defence system resulted in such losses to our bombers that by the end of 1941 … the decision was taken to restrict operations over Germany until the spring of the following year.

Yet even then, throughout 1942 the Kammhuber Line continued to increase both in its depth – with deepening 'fighter belts' around the coasts of Belgium, Holland and north-west Germany – and length, with extensions towards Paris and northern Denmark. Although the British, owing to scientist Professor R. V. Jones' work, had made considerable progress in mapping the location and extent of the Kammhuber Line by March 1943, it had become clear that if Bomber Command was to not tackle it head-on – which itself was increasingly dangerous – then the alternative was flying long detours around it, with its trade-off between fuel-load and bomb-load. It therefore seemed that in the skies over Western Europe, the Germans had secured the upper-hand through this elaborate, expensively equipped and significantly manned air defence line. The Luftwaffe's signal service (*Nachtrichtentruppe*) was moreover able to obtain indications that an operation was likely by detecting the transmissions made by H2S and wireless equipment that were tested on the pre-operation Night Flying Tests.

Patrolling the Kammhuber Line were of course the Luftwaffe's night fighters. This had started in June 1940 from aircrew in ZG-1, which had been retained in the Low Countries for training in night flying. In addition, trainees were personally recruited from the Fighter School at München-Schleissheim by Major Wolfgang Falck, who became known as the 'Father of Night Fighting' and whose surname (meaning falcon) was adopted as the unit's crest. Working on the tactics of night fighting, Falck's *Nacht und Versuchs Staffel* (Night and Experimental Squadron) was renamed Gruppe I of Nachtjagdgeschwader 1 (I/NJG-1) on 20 July 1940, following Kammhuber's appointment to head the Luftwaffe's night fighter arm three-days earlier, and comprised 23 Bf 110s. The NJG was the core unit of the night fighter arm, containing some 30–50 twin-engined aircraft divided into three of four Gruppen, usually stationed on their own airfields. NJG-1 became the seasoned veterans of the night fighter arm, and its pilots – especially such aces as Werner Streib, Heinz-Wolfgang Schnaufer, Hans-Joachim Jabs and Helmut Lent – would shoot down considerable numbers of British bombers during the Battle

A Flak gun crew preparing to fire. The picture gives a good idea about how searchlights were used collectively to form 'cones' in the sky to highlight a British bomber before the German AA guns would open fire. A noticeable feature of bombing raids was how the co-ordination of searchlights and flak defences lessened as the attack went on, remaining either stationary or moving around erratically with the flak being fired in barrage form. This was all part of Bomber Command's tactics of swamping German air defences through the concentrated bomber stream. (Getty Images)

ABOVE A GROUND-CONTROLLED INTERCEPTION (GCI) UNDER THE KAMMHUBER AIR-DEFENCE SYSTEM IN 1943

1 In the morning before an operation, British bomber crews embark on an air test to check their aircraft's performance and systems. Particularly tested are the bomber's navigation systems and wireless equipment, but this gives off electronic emissions that are picked up by personnel of the *Nachtrichtentruppe*, the German signal service. This gives the Luftwaffe advanced warning that a British night operation is highly likely.

2 Once underway, the British bomber formation is detected first by Freya long-range radars and then by the Giant Würzburg sets, which provide early warning to the ground-control intercept stations who then track a specific British bomber.

3 The British bomber is monitored by the staff on a plotting room within the ground control station ('T-hut'), also the German night fighter waiting to intercept, on a specially designed instrument called a 'Seeburg Table'. This saw the positions of the bomber and fighter projected onto the table by spots of coloured light; red for the bomber and blue for the night fighter. These projections were moved following instructions given on the telephone to the operators of the Giant Würzburgs.

4 The German night fighter orbits a radio beacon located in its 'box' (in order to prevent the aircraft from straying out of its assigned *Raum*) and awaits precise information from its ground controllers on the bomber's location, speed and altitude. With that information, the German night fighter begins to stalk the British bomber. The quality of the system and the frequently given information allows the German night fighter to be guided to within 400 yards of its target, before its airborne radar or the crew's visual sighting takes over.

5 Using its Lichtenstein radar, developed by the Telefunken firm, the night fighter homes in on the British bomber, seeing the red glow from its exhaust manifold, and commences its attack. Having shot down its assigned target, the night fighter would often find other British bombers in the vicinity and attack these. Consequently, British losses could often occur within minutes of each other – victims of the same night fighter crew. The British bombers, meanwhile, would continue on to the Ruhr with its mighty flak defences, knowing that the Luftwaffe now knew their heading, speed and altitude.

of the Ruhr. This was because of NJG-1's location in the critical area of the Low Countries, right on the bombers' route to and from Germany. NJG-1 would also be joined by NJG-3 (stationed in north-west Germany and Denmark) and NJG-4 (based in Belgium and northern France). The newly formed NJG-5 was based around Berlin, and from May 1943, NJG-6 was being established in southern Germany. Finally, spring 1943 saw NJG-2 re-forming in Holland (having been weakened by its battles in the Mediterranean), some of its Gruppen would be operationally active during the Battle of the Ruhr. In expanding the number of NJG, many of the experienced pilots from NJG-1 were transferred to lead these new units, which was indicative of the growing number of aircraft:115 in September 1940 to 345 two years later, then 490 by spring 1943, representing the majority of Germany's twin-engined fighter production being consumed by the Luftwaffe's night fighter arm (designated from August 1941 as Fliegerkorps XI).

Notwithstanding the radar and communications technology of the Kammhuber Line, there was one thing missing: airborne radars carried on the Luftwaffe's night fighter itself. Such a device had had a tortuous development since summer 1940. Very quickly, Falck believed night fighters needed equipment to aid detection, for reliance solely on searchlights or visual contact remained unsatisfactory. Moreover, whilst the GCI system could vector a night fighter onto a target, an airborne radar was needed for the final 400–500 yards before interception. By mid-1941, the Telefunken firm had produced an AI (airborne interception) set called the Lichtenstein. Nicknamed the 'barbed wire' by German aircrews, the antennae's effect on aircraft performance, with a 25mph speed reduction caused by drag, meant many pilots initially chose to fly aircraft without it. However, by March 1943, an overwhelming number of night fighters were equipped with it, owing to the development of lighter aerials that had a less detrimental effect on the aircraft's performance.

AI also provided a 'what might have been' story for the Luftwaffe in spring and summer 1943. I/NJG-2, formed in Düsseldorf during summer 1940 from twin-engined fighter units that had participated in the campaigns against Norway and the Low Countries (ZG.76 and ZKG.30), soon operated from a base at Gilze Rijen (Holland). Its Ju 88s or Do 17s undertook 'intruder' operations, catching Bomber Command's aircraft near their home bases or over the Channel. Kammhuber saw this activity as a valuable addition to Germany's air defences, and the unit would be increased to 53 aircraft by March 1941. But NJG-2's intruder activities were swiftly terminated the following autumn when Hitler ordered its dispatch to the Mediterranean, in a clear indication of the stretching demands on German resources from fighting in multiple theatres. Doing so represented a lost opportunity, and allowed Bomber Command to fly in UK skies without casualties being inflicted on it by the Luftwaffe.

Nonetheless, the Luftwaffe was well placed to provide stiff opposition to Bomber Command's operations in spring 1943, with its ground-radars, plotting tables, GCI systems, airborne radars and experienced aircrews. Yet as capable as they were, the air defences had weaknesses. The increasing American daylight offensive caused the Luftwaffe, which was becoming short of day fighters, to use its night fighters in the daylight role. There was more than a hint of desperation in this, especially as the specialist technology and training on which night fighting depended was being expended in attritional battles with the US Eighth. Indeed, responding to threats in an improvised way, the Luftwaffe would, after Bomber Command's introduction of Window, use single-engine fighters at night – an indication of the Germans' increasing desperation. Not surprisingly, pressed into action during day and night, aircrew fatigue became a problem, with all the detrimental effects on efficiency and likelihood of flying accidents. The tiring daily life of a German pilot manning the Kammhuber Line proves a consistent theme in Wilhelm Johnen's account, with the operations in combating the round-the-clock bombing all too visibly straining the pilots' faces. 'Tired and sleepy', he described:

the crews slumped in their armchairs. Chess boards lay abandoned and only soft music could be heard on the wireless during the night hours. The hands of the clock wandered towards 02.00 hours. A few of the crews had retired to their bunks in full flying kit, ready at any moment to scramble … Some of the men had fallen asleep with their heads on the table, and one pilot was still holding the book he had been reading when he dozed off.

Not helping matters was the continuation of the debate on aircraft production priorities, and whether the emphasis should be on fighters for defence or bombers for attack. Because of this, opportunities were not seized quickly and the new purpose-built night fighter called the He 219 'Uhu' ('Owl'), which had had significant input from Kammhuber and Night Fighter Command and combined high speed, good range, excellent visibility and heavy armament, was developed far too slowly.

Beyond this, the Kammhuber Line suffered two serious drawbacks, one tactical and the other technical. With regards to the latter, the system suffered from considerable rigidity in its operation, with units strictly limited to their own box. On the tactical side, the British gradually undid the Kammhuber Line in two ways. In June 1942, the 'Thousand-Bomber' attack on Cologne revealed the advantages of a concentrated bomber stream in both getting through the Kammhuber Line and saturating the target's air defences. Yet the regime's continued focus on retaliation and the ebbing away of the British bombing offensive during autumn 1942 lulled Hitler and the Nazi leadership into a false sense of security. The Kammhuber Line's obvious weakness was simply forgotten, with its sheer depth and sophistication simply presumed to be enough. This was a mistake, for the concentrated bomber stream became the standard tactic of Bomber Command during the Battle of the Ruhr precisely because the British had developed a clearer understanding of how Kammhuber's system worked during autumn 1942. The link between a box's ground control and the waiting night fighter could be overwhelmed by sizeable numbers of British aircraft travelling through it at any one time. The Germans did react by deploying a greater number of radars so a single ground-control station could operate three night fighters simultaneously, and by enhancing the radio capabilities so information about British aircraft movements could be passed on to the ground controllers of adjacent boxes, but such improvements remained insufficient. Sometimes called 'swamping', this method meant less time for interceptions as the bombers traversed the Kammhuber Line much more quickly, whilst with the ground controller concentrating on one British aircraft, many others could simultaneously get through unscathed. Kammhuber attempted to counter this development by making the air defence boxes in depth but, as a post-war study by the Air Ministry noted, this only caused the system to become 'very uneconomical, since it necessitated the wide dispersal of fighters over the whole defensive belt, of which only a few could be brought into play against any one threat'. Thus, even before 24–25 July 1943, when the British deployed the decisive blow of Window, the Kammhuber Line was losing efficiency and living on borrowed time. Indeed, the Germans themselves seemed to be recognizing this, for in early July the Luftwaffe was pioneering a method much less dependent on ground control, the *Wilde Sau* ('Wild Boar') tactic where interception took place using the bright light of the target area.

Though the Window story has been central to accounts of the Battle of Hamburg, this counter-measure did feature in the Battle of the Ruhr's final stages, on the operations to Essen on 25–26 July and Remscheid on 30–31 July. Window meant Kammhuber's expensive air defence system, having consumed considerable investment of resources, technology and

The former bomber pilot, Hajo Herrmann. His new tactics of *Wilde Sau*, in which night fighters – often the single-engined interceptors of the Bf 109 and Fw 190 – attacked British bombers around the target using the illumination of fires and searchlights, was increasingly used in the later stages of the Battle of the Ruhr, especially on the Cologne operations of 3–4 and 8–9 July. It became the standard, indeed the only, method of night fighting after Bomber Command's use of *Window* against Hamburg several weeks later until well into the winter of 1943–4. (Bundesarchiv, Bild 146-1985-015-20, Fotograf(in): Hoffmann)

manpower, had become redundant. The simple counter-measure of Window, having been held in Britain's inventory for some time, 'blinded' the Würzburg ground-radars and thus rendered the GCI system, on which the operation of the Kammhuber Line so critically depended, useless. In essence, the Kammhuber Line, the AHB concluded, had become 'an expensive and useless luxury overnight'. Yet notwithstanding its abrupt ending, the Kammhuber Line had proved a considerable obstacle for Bomber Command over the previous two years, and had inflicted high losses on the British during the Battle of the Ruhr, even in its final weeks with costly operations in June and July.

Flak

The ferocity of the flak defences of the Ruhr left an unforgettable mark on many Bomber Command airmen. In terms of sheer numbers, the Ruhr was one of the most heavily defended places in Germany; moreover, its overlapping urban areas meant the flak defences of one place could be used to shoot down bombers attacking somewhere else, even if Air Vice-Marshal Ralph Cochrane later told Harris that 'although the Ruhr is defended by an astronomical number of guns, the density at any one spot does not appear to be higher than at Munich or Schweinfurt'.

Nonetheless, Germany's flak defences required ever increasing amounts of resources and manpower, with 439,500 personnel in 1942 rising to 642,700 in 1943. This increase certainly reflected Hitler's lowering confidence in Göring's Luftwaffe, and also a belief that, for the Germans on the ground, flak guns seemed good for morale even if the results achieved were modest. Historian Williamson Murray writes how 'antiaircraft guns, blasting into the night, provided the population with a psychological crutch no matter how ineffective the weapons might be'. Achieving this increase came about in two ways. First, flak units were soon being withdrawn from the fronts to bolster Germany's defences. Back in December 1942, for example, some 150 flak and searchlight batteries had been sent, on the personal order of Hitler, to strengthen Italy's air defences, but were returned to Germany during spring 1943 when the bombing was clearly becoming more intense. Second, increased production saw some 30–40 heavy batteries (ten light batteries and 12 searchlight batteries) being made per month.

In terms of organization, flak was expanded into Grossbatterien, which oversaw two or three single batteries, often defending large and important targets, and crucially selecting

The commander-in-chief of the Luftwaffe, Reichsmarschall Hermann Göring confers with Hitler and Speer in August 1943. Following Stalingrad, Göring became seriously out of favour with Hitler, as Goebbels' diary entries frequently stated. Then came Bomber Command's destruction of Speer's factories in the Ruhr and Hamburg, which Göring's air force seemed largely powerless to resist. (Bundesarchiv, Bild 146-1977-149-13, Fotograf(in): Hoffmann, Heinrich)

An impressive side-profile of the 88mm Flak gun. The Ruhr cities, towns and industries were defended by hundreds of these weapons. (Getty Images)

their own targets in contrast to the previous system of 'sector defence'. This had involved flak and searchlights being allocated to defend a specific zone of a city, with a sector often comprising a maximum of 30 searchlights and some 60 heavy and light flak guns. All the searchlights would 'cone' a single aircraft, and all guns would then fire into the apex of the searchlights where the targeted bomber was located. It was because of this that many British airmen remember the multiple beams of light, which seemed to turn darkness into day if caught, sometimes this approach could work. One Pathfinder pilot recalled that a succession of target-marking aircraft were clearly picked out, held by the searchlights and fired upon. The destruction of target markers no doubt affected the accuracy and concentration of the subsequent British attack, but, as terrifying as this was, it meant that only one aircraft suffered at any one time, whilst the bomber stream, concentrated in both time and space, saw successive numbers of bombers carry on unimpeded to the target. This meant the ground defences became 'swamped' by the sheer number of British bombers, before becoming more ineffective once the bombs began to drop. Consequently, as the Battle of the Ruhr progressed, so German flak defences were thoroughly reorganized, with this old method of 'sector defence' superseded by the Grossbatterien. Moreover, a single battery increased from six to eight guns (up to 12 in 1944), with up to 16 searchlights, and these fixed flak defences were bolstered by 88s mounted on railway bogeys that could be moved quickly to supplement a city's defences, especially one that seemed a particular focus of British attention. Through these measures, the Ruhr's air defences were quickly strengthened during spring 1943, whilst the 88s were augmented by increasing numbers of 105mm and 128mm guns.

Yet as the British Bombing Survey Unit (BBSU) noted, flak gun production in 1943–44 represented some 25–30 per cent of German weapons manufacture, with flak shells being some 15–20 per cent of the total ammunition produced. Thus, the amount of industrial effort needed to produce these items was in exchange for only a modest return of bombers shot down (though a considerable number of British aircraft did return with varying amounts of damage). Once Window had 'blinded' the radars needed by the flak gunners for predicted fire, the German defence had to resort to box-barrage firing that consumed huge quantities of ammunition that Germany's hard-pressed armaments industry had to replace. At a time of increasing battles of attrition on the land fronts in Russia and the Mediterranean, this was a high price to pay for defending German skies, yet one that paradoxically seemed absolutely necessary to defend Germany's war economy.

CAMPAIGN OBJECTIVES
The Reich's industrial heartland and its workers

The Ruhr cities, towns and industries

Dissected by several rivers – the Rhine, Ruhr and Wupper – the Ruhr area measured some 40 miles from east to west and on average 25 miles from north to south, and thus covered an area of around 1,000 square miles. Within it, the suburbs of its principal towns often ran into one another, causing continuous bands of heavily built-up areas, home to a pre-war population of 4.1m. There were important reasons why this area became the foremost industrial area of Germany. The Ruhr was rich in coking coal, supplying about 70 per cent of Germany's total supply, and from this stemmed a giant steel industry developed in the area, producing over 60 per cent of Germany's wartime pig iron and steel requirements. Coal and steel production gave rise to heavy engineering industries being founded in the Ruhr, including the famous arms-makers Krupps of Essen and Rheinmetall-Borsig in Düsseldorf. Thus, given its raw materials, ready access to water, plentiful labour and its established heavy industries, the Ruhr was largely a self-supporting area. As noted by HQ Bomber Command, this meant 'the concentrated industrial activity of this area is without parallel in this country or anywhere in Europe'.

By 1945, the Ruhr had had some 123,000 tonnes of bombs dropped on it by Bomber Command alone. Such a figure was a consequence of the long-held perception of the vital need to bomb this industrial area, which predated the outbreak of war in September 1939.

Notwithstanding its very modest capabilities in 1939–40, Bomber Command was confident it could destroy the Ruhr, particularly by focusing on the bombing of 19 power-stations and 26 coking plants. Incredibly, it believed the region 'could be put out of action in a fortnight' by making 3,000 sorties, reducing Germany's war production 'almost to a standstill'. The Air Ministry thought this too optimistic, and its Air Targets Sub-Committee examined other ways of damaging the Ruhr, by attacking the Möhne and Sorpe Dams, the canals leading to and from the region and its railway communications.

A typical scene from Germany, showing a picturesque and compact city centre surrounded by residential districts in close proximity to areas of heavy industry. This is Bochum in the 1920s. (Getty Images)

OPPOSITE THE RUHR–RHINELAND: CITIES, INDUSTRIES AND TRANSPORTATION

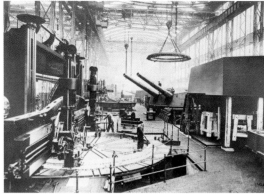

ABOVE LEFT
The home of German arms production, the giant Krupp Works of Essen. (Getty Images)

ABOVE RIGHT
Krupps produced heavy guns of all calibres, including those for naval and coastal turrets as depicted here. (Getty Images)

Though undertaken subsequently, these plans were too ambitious for the modest capabilities of Bomber Command in 1939–40. Moreover, it remained open to question whether the bombers could operate efficiently from bases in France or whether their aircraft could overfly Belgium before it was invaded. The French, during the Phoney War, also had objections to bombing the Ruhr for fear of inviting German bombing attacks on France.

On 9 July 1941, a greater focus on the Ruhr–Rhineland was ordered, but this was to be undertaken against the region's main railway centres in Cologne (Kalk-Nord), Duisburg (Hochfeld-Sud), Düsseldorf (Derendorf), Duisburg (Ruhrort), Hamm, Osnabrück, Soest and Schwerte, targets that were important for Germany's wider transportation system. Only when this transportation Directive was superseded by the 14 February 1942 Directive – called by the BBSU Report on a number of occasions the 'Towns Directif' – were four Ruhr–Rhineland cities (Cologne, Essen, Duisburg and Düsseldorf) placed as Bomber Command's first-priority targets because of their industrial importance in Germany's war economy.

LARGE RUHR CITIES			
Target (codename)	Approx pop size	Description of importance:	Total Key-Point Rating (KPR)
Bochum (Quinnat)	305,000 (MEW's British equivalent: Hull)	Coal Mining, Coke, Steel, Special High-Grade Steels, Benzine, Railway Equipment, Transportation Vereinigte Stahlwerke AG (Bochumer Verein Weke Gusstahlfabrik) (Priority 1+) Vereinigte Stahlwerke AG (Bochumer Verein Werk Stahl Industrie) (Priority 1) Vereinigte Stahlwerke AG (Bochumer Verein Werk Hontrop) (Priority 1) Vereinigte Stahlwerke AG (Bochumer Verein Werk Weitmar) (Priority 1) Eisen und Hüttenwerke AG (Priority 1) Krupp Treibst Offwerke GmbH (Priority 1) Maschinen und Bahndarf AG(Priority 2) Gelsenkirchener Bergwerk AG (Carolinen Gluck Pit) (Priority 1) Friedrich Krupp AG Hannover Pits I/II/V (Priority 1) Bergbau AG Lothringen Ver. President I//II/IV Pits (Priority 2) Weitmar M/Y* (3,100) Bochum-Reimke M/Y (3,200) Bohcum-Langendreer M/Y (5,000) Bohcum-Dahlhausen M/Y (3,600) Vereinigte Stahlwerke railway sidings Bahnhof Nord railway station	174

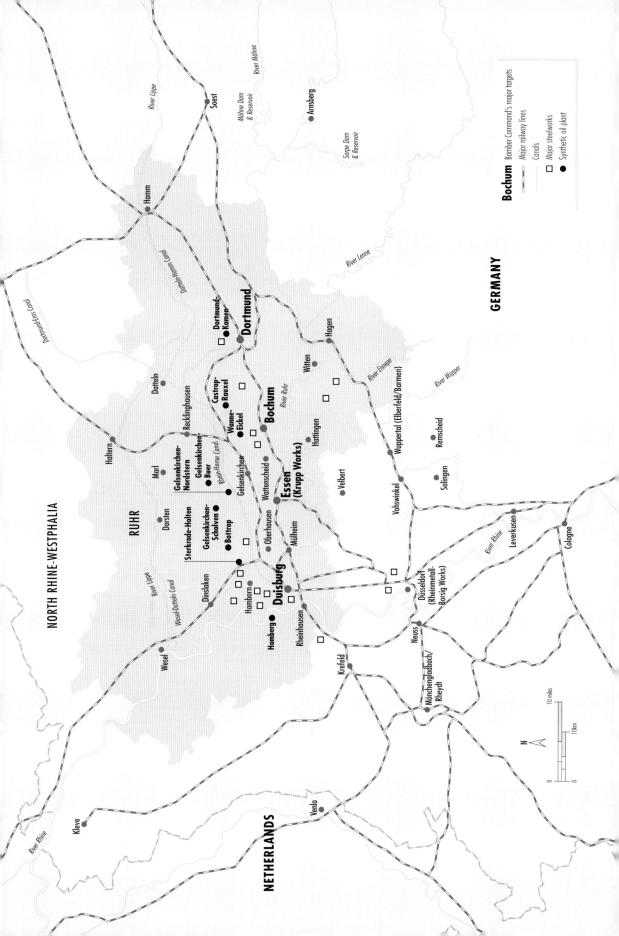

NORTH RHINE-WESTPHALIA

GERMANY

NETHERLANDS

RUHR

Bochum Bomber Command's major targets
— Major railway lines
— Canals
☐ Major steelworks
● Synthetic oil plant

River Lippe

River Möhne

Möhne Dam & Reservoir

Sorpe Dam & Reservoir

Soest

Arnsberg

Hamm

Datteln-Hamm Canal

Dortmund-Ems Canal

River Lippe

Wesel-Datteln Canal

River Lenne

Dortmund-Kamen

Dortmund

Recklinghausen

Haltern

Marl

Dorsten

Castrop-Rauxel

Wanne-Eickel

Gelsenkirchen-Nordstern

Gelsenkirchen-Buer

Rhein-Herne Canal

Gelsenkirchen-Scholven

Sterkrade-Holten

Bottrop

Gelsenkirchen

Wattenscheid

Bochum

Witten

River Ruhr

Hagen

River Ennepe

River Wupper

Essen (Krupp Works)

Oberhausen

Mülheim

Hattingen

Velbert

Wuppertal (Elberfeld/Barmen)

Remscheid

Solingen

Vohswinkel

Dinslaken

Hamborn

Duisburg

Rheinhausen

Homberg

Wesel

River Lippe

Leverkusen

Cologne

River Rhine

Düsseldorf (Rheinmetall-Borsig Works)

Neuss

Krefeld

Mönchengladbach/Rheydt

Kleve

Venlo

River Rhine

N

0   10 miles
0   10km

Dortmund (Sprat)	542,000 (Edinburgh)	Steel, Coal Mining, Synthetic Oil, Transportation Vereinigte Stahlwerke AG (Dortmunder Union Bruckenbrau AG) (Priority 1+) Hoesch Eisen & Stahlwerke AG (Priority 1+) Hoesch AG Kaiserstuhl Mine (Priority 2) Gelsenkirchener Bergwerke AG (Priority 2) Dortmund Ewing M/Y (2,000) Dortmund Süd M/Y (2,400) Dortmund Verschiebahnhof M/Y (4,800) Dortmunderfeld M/Y (3,000) Dortmund-Ems Canal terminus	110
Duisburg (Cod)	435,000 (Sheffield)	Iron & Steel, Coal Mining, Coke, Synthetic Oil, Transportation Vereinigte Stahlwerke AG Hutte Ruhrort-Meiderich (Priority 1+) Vereinigte Stahlwerke AG Wannheim (Priority 1+) Vereinigte Stahlwerke AG Niederheintsche Hutte (Priority 1+) Gelsenkirchener Bergwerke AG (Priority 1) August Thyssen Hütte AG (Priority 1+) Deutsche Eisenwerk AG (Priority 1) Deutsche Röhrenwerk AG (Priority 1) Bandeisenwalzwerke AG (Priority 2) Ruhrchemie AG (Priority 2) Homberg synthetic oil plant (200,000 tons p.a.) Ruhrort-Hafen-neu-Schultenhof M/Y (5,000) Wedau M/Y (7,200) Duisburg Hauptbahnhof M/Y (3,600) Duisburg-Hochfeld-Süd M/Y (2,600) Duisburg-Ruhrort inland port area	239
Essen (Bullhead)	1,139,000 (inc wider district) (Manchester)	Heavy Engineering, Armaments, Locomotives, Armour Plate, Turbines, Zinc Smelting, Transportation Krupp Main Works (Priority 1+) Krupp Stahlwerke AG (Priority 1) Th. Goldschmidt (Priority 3) AG des Altenbergs für bergbau (Priority 2) Zinkhüttenbetrieb (Priority 2) Presswerk AG (Priority 3) Essen-Frintrop M/Y (5,400) Essen-Verschiebe M/Y (2,600) Essen-Kupferdreh M/Y (2,600)	812
Gelsenkirchen (Ferox)	317,000 (Bradford)	Synthetic Oil, Coal Mining, Transportation Gelsenkirchen-Nordstern synthetic oil plant (325,000 tons p.a.) Gelsenkirchen-Buer synthetic oil plant (350,000 tons p.a.) Wanne-Eickel synthetic oil plant (130,000 tons p.a.) Gelsenkirchen-Schalke M/Y (2,200) Herne M/Y (2,400) Wanne-Eickel M/Y (2,500)	56

*'M/Y' = Marshalling Yard. The numbers refer to how many wagons the yard could store.

However there were limits on the influence of the Ministry of Economic Warfare (MEW) when it came to advocating placing Bomber Command's aiming-points over precise industries. Indeed, Portal, the Chief of the Air Staff, felt compelled to clarify that it was the city itself, not specific factories or areas of industrial activity, that was the primary consideration. On 15 February, he informed Air Chief Marshal Norman Bottomley, Deputy Chief of the Air Staff that 'the aiming-points are to be the built-up areas, not, for instance, the dockyards or aircraft factories... This must be made quite clear.'

Nonetheless, the MEW did devise a rating-system for Germany's towns and cities in order to measure their respective economic importance. This was the 'Key-Point Rating' (KPR) system, which Bufton defined as 'a convenient means of measuring the overall importance to the German war effort of individual towns as a whole'. Such information was enshrined in the MEW's 'guidebook' to targets in Germany known as the 'Bomber's Baedeker'. Comprising two volumes (A–K and L–Z), arranged alphabetically was every town with a population of over 15,000 people (although suburbs and satellite towns were incorporated into the entry for the larger cities) thus the entire Ruhr was presented under the four main cities of Bochum, Dortmund, Duisburg and Essen. Most significantly, KPRs were assigned to specific installations according to their importance under the headings of 'factories', 'public utilities' and 'transportation facilities'. In the case of factories, for example, the grading system was:

1+ Factories of leading importance in the German war effort.

1. Major plants in major industries.

2. Minor plants in major industries or major plants in minor industries.

3. Factories of small importance in the German war effort.

Not surprisingly, the Ruhr contained a considerable number of 1+ rated industrial targets. Moreover, the area's huge concentration of steelworks, coal mines, massive factories, railway lines, inland ports and workers' housing all meant the Ruhr was particularly susceptible to the 'bludgeon' of area attack.

Given the Ruhr's many important targets, it was small wonder that Bomber Command developed the approach of area bombing, which had itself come about because of the British bomber force's weaknesses in navigation and bombing accuracy. As Harris wrote after the war:

The limitations … on bombing accuracy largely controlled the choice of targets, since large industrial areas were more suitable for heavy attacks than individual factories and plants. This policy, although based on the meagre chances of direct hits on small targets except under most favourable conditions, was also supported by a study of the results of German night attacks on this country, which indicated that the quickest and most economical way of achieving the aims of the offensive was to devastate in turn the large industrial cities of Germany.

Yet 11 months later, the situation was quite different. Harris now led an expanded bomber force, especially in four-engined 'heavies', and was operating alongside an American bomber force which, if still weak, was at least beginning to bomb Germany. Both strategic bomber forces were, moreover, operating to a new Directive that stipulated a combined Anglo–American 'round-the-clock' bombing campaign against the German war economy. Known as the Casablanca Directive, this saw the target of lowering workers' morale – now designated as 'undermining' it so the German people's 'capacity for armed resistance is fatally weakened' – joined by the aim of the 'general disorganization' of German war industry. As Harris commented, this 'gave me a very wide range of choice and allowed me to attack pretty well any German industrial city of 100,000 inhabitants or above'. 'But', he continued, 'the Ruhr remained a principal objective because it was the most important industrial area in the whole of Germany.' This, then, was the instruction by which the Battle of the Ruhr commenced some weeks later, and in continuity with the earlier Directive, Essen was the place where it all began.

Essen had received eight attacks in March–April 1942, and five more in June, with one being a 'Thousand-Bomber' raid under Operation *Millennium*, during what could be termed as the 'first' Battle of the Ruhr. It then received six heavy attacks in 1943, and many more thereafter. It was an industrial target worthy of the attention.

Essen contained sprawling suburbs, but also a large number of industrial workers and dwellings tightly packed into a compact area surrounding as an Air Ministry assessment states 'the great armaments centre of the Ruhr'. Krupps was a sprawling complex of factories

OPPOSITE ESSEN: THE PRIZE TARGET FOR BOMBER COMMAND

devoted to different industrial activities by 1939 which occupied a 2,150-acre site in the western part of the city centre. The Krupp Works was so large that it was considered to be Essen itself and this had a unique bearing on the precise aiming-point when attacking the city. The site contained numerous large and small workshops for producing variously sized components in steel, 120 steam hammers and 11 steam-hydraulic presses, two 100-ton cranes to handle large pieces of steel, and several steel and iron rolling mills. By 1939, it also produced locomotives, railway wagons and lorries; indeed, the northern portion of the Krupps site contained the largest locomotive works in Europe. Krupp was no longer just a vast arsenal but a series of factories producing such materiel as armour plate, parts for turbines and components for lorries and trains, although it did produce armaments that required heavy engineering, such as large-calibre guns and turrets. Even though Krupps covered a huge area, Essen and its surrounding districts did contain other war industries, including the zinc smelters of AG des Altenbergs für bergbau and Zinkhüttenbetrieb in the Borbeck district and the plastics works of Presswerk AG. Overall, approximately 210,000 people, from a pre-war population of 1.1 million, were engaged in war production.

West of Essen was the sprawling industrial town of Duisburg, which was notable for the waterways running through it: the rivers Rhine (from north to south) and Ruhr (from east to west) and the Rhein–Herne Canal, which linked Duisburg to Dortmund. Inhabited by a population of 440,000, Duisburg's heavily built-up areas lay either side of the Ruhr, comprising the satellite towns of Dinslaken, Hamborn, Ruhrort and Rheinhausen. The area's waterborne and railway transportation made the entire area an important target. Moreover, the area's large coal deposits had led to the development of Duisburg's sizeable iron and steel industries, in which coal was also converted into coke and gas products. One RAAF document stated:

> Duisburg, which might be called the Sheffield of Germany, contains a large variety of industries, even for the Ruhr; apart from Berlin, it is by far the most active industrial centre in the Reich … Steel works, armament factories, synthetic oilworks [sic], metal works, coking plants and chemical works are packed together in an area seven miles long and three miles wide.

This extensive industrial activity had also led to the development of a vast railway network and marshalling yards, and at Hamborn, to the largest inland port in Europe, which handled some 75 per cent of all Rhine cargoes. In a briefing document for Operation *Millennium Two* (Duisburg was designated the alternative target for the primary one of Bremen), HQ Bomber Command stated that Duisburg's 'elimination would have the most serious consequences for the duration of the war however long'. Though Essen was synonymous with Krupp's industrial empire, it was hard not to argue that Duisburg was a target of equal importance.

In the opposite direction, some miles east of Essen lay another important target, the town of Bochum, whose industrial activities were very similar to Duisburg's. The MoHS (Ministry of Home Security), which also examined the effects of bombing on Germany and the industrial and residential nature of targets there, observed that Bochum was:

Powering Germany's steel and arms production was the Ruhr area's extensive coal deposits. Mining was particularly centred round Bochum and also Wattenscheid, as depicted here, where a farmer tends to his crops. (Getty Images)

Gelsenkirchen

River Ruhr

Essen

Rhine-Herne Canal

Oberhausen

Emscher Canal

Mülheim

River Ruhr

Site of Krupp Works
Built-up towns
Built-up suburbs
Bomber Command's aiming-point over the Krupp Works
Major railway lines

N

1 mile

1km

0

0

The ironworks at Oberhausen, an industrial town between Duisburg and Essen. The important inland waterway of the Rhein-Herne Canal can be seen on the left. (Getty Images)

The centre of that part of the steel industry which specialized in the production of high grade steels for armaments, and as a centre of the Ruhr coal industry. The major industrial area is compact and lies to the west of, and immediately adjacent to, the main town, which consisted of a heavily built-up area which had grown up around the site of a medieval town.

Though the smallest in size and population (320,000) of the big four Ruhr cities, Bochum, in the eastern part of the central Ruhr, was in fact, according to the MoHS, 'the centre of the production of one-third of the whole Ruhr output of coal'. In a 500-acre area were the three huge steelworks of Bochumer Verein, which were owned by the Vereinigte Stahlwerke and produced one million tons of steel and pig iron per year. One of these plants, together with the smaller steelworks of Eisen und Hüttenwerke AG, produced high-grade alloy steels ('special steels') particularly needed for guns, aircraft, aero-engines and machine tools. Bochum's large coal production was also important for industries located in other parts of the Ruhr and further into Germany, which meant Bochum had developed as a large railway centre with several marshalling yards; the city was also surrounded by several satellite towns containing important industries.

Steel production produced by the huge conglomerate, *Vereinigte Stahlwerke AG*. This combine possessed many sites around the Ruhr, three in Bochum alone, in addition to this one located in Dortmund. (Getty Images)

The Ruhr region also contained, in Harris' words, 'one of the most important centres of heavy industry in Germany' – Dortmund. Within this largest city of the Ruhr, which had a population of 550,000 lay a number of steelworks and synthetic oil plants. Dortmund was a significant railway centre because of its location in the east of the Ruhr, and it was where the Dortmund–Ems canal started, which was 170 miles long and connected with the River Ems and the North Sea.

Another notable target was Krefeld. On the left bank of the Rhine, this city was located south-west of Duisburg on the western outskirts of the Ruhr

With a population of 170,000, Krefeld's industrial importance lay in its high-grade steel production by the Deutsche Edelstahlwerke conglomerate (some 200,000 tons per-year) – the largest manufacturer of this material in Germany – which was then supplied to such firms as Krupps and Rheinmentall-Borsig for use in the manufacture of guns, aero-engine crankshafts, machine tools and other metal components that had to withstand heat. Krefeld was also a centre of silk manufacture, which, in war production, was a vital fabric for parachutes.

Finally, there was Wuppertal (Barmen/Elberfeld) – which Harris described as a 'second-class target' – and the similarly small Ruhr towns of Hagen, Hamm, Mülheim, Oberhausen, Remscheid, Solingen and Witten.

The proximity of heavy industry and the railway network can be seen clearly in this photograph of Dortmund's steelworks. This was a scene typical throughout much of the Ruhr region. (Getty Images)

SMALLER RUHR TOWNS			
Target (codename)	Approx pop size	Description of importance	Total Key-Point Rating (KPR)
Hagen (Rainbow)	152,000 (MEW's British equivalent: Cardiff)	Special High-Grade Steels, U-Boat Electric Motors and Batteries, Transportation Accumulatoren Fabrik AG (Priority 1+) Hagen-Vorhalle M/Y (3,800) Hagen-Henstey M/Y (2,350)	71
Krefeld (Mahseer)	171,000 (Leeds)	Special High-Grade Steels, Silk Deutsche Edelstahlwerke (Priority 1+) Uerdingen M/Y (2,500)	36
Mülheim (Steelhead)	137,000 (Wolverhampton)	Special High-Grade Steels, Steel Ingots, Pig-Iron, Coke Verein Stahlwerke (Priority 1+) August Thyssen Hütte (Priority 1) Friedrich Wilhelmshütte Iron Foundry (Priority 2) Mülheim-Ruhr-Speldorf M/Y (3,000)	48
Oberhausen (Gillaroo)	192,000 (Plymouth)	Iron and Steel, Coke, Synthetic Oil, Transportation Gutehoffnungshutte AG (Priority 1) Deutsche Babcock and Wilcox (Priority 2) Sterkrade-Holten synthetic oil plant (130,000 tons p.a.) Oberhausen West M/Y (3,100) Rhein–Herne Canal Emscher Canal	48
Remscheid (Chavendor)	105,000 (St Helens)	Precision and Machine Tools H. Alexanderswerk AG (Priority 1)	18
Wuppertal (Barmen / Elberfeld) (Sprod)	402,000 (Coventry/ Sunderland)	Light Engineering, Ball Bearings, Railway Axles, Components, Chemicals, Dyes, Pharmaceuticals IG Farben (Elberfeld) (Priority 2) Jaeger (Elberfeld) (Priority 2) Wuppertal-Vohwinkel M/Y (2,800)	33

Industrial workers and morale

A more generalized approach of destroying cities and, of course, 'neutralizing' the other critical element of the industrial workers (through either de-housing or killing), was reflected in the Casablanca Directive of 14 February 1942 which told Bomber Command 'to focus attacks on the morale of the enemy civil population, and, in particular, of the industrial workers'. 'My primary authorized task was therefore clear beyond doubt', Harris wrote, 'to inflict the most severe material damage on German industrial cities', which was itself 'a formidable task' given Bomber Command's capabilities and numbers in early-1942.

Bomber Command had been conducting attacks against German civilian morale since summer 1941. Harris later described the attacks on morale as 'a counsel of despair, based on the previous failure of night bombing, and the breakdown of the theory of precision attacks on key factories', reflecting an 'unbounded optimism' as to what strategic bombing could actually achieve. Nonetheless, morale was a target that remained 'stuck in the system'.

The Casablanca Directive instructed Bomber Command to undertake the disorganization of German war industry, and though the morale of industrial workers was no longer stated directly, it remained an unstated goal of the area offensive. It was not for nothing that continued assessments, analyses and reports made by the MEW, the MoHS and the Air Ministry's Directorate of Bomber Operations continued to reference the population size of German cities, their geographical dimensions and the population density.

Area bombing was the 'catch-all' strategy of hindering German war production that included not just the destruction of factories but also of local housing, transportation and public utilities – anything that adversely affected the worker's ability to produce.

The breached Möhne Dam. The height of the dam wall and the low water level give an idea of just how much water was lost through this attack. The escaping torrents flooded the German countryside, but achievement of the true aim of depriving the Ruhr's war industries and towns of precious water supplies is more debatable. (Bundesarchiv, Bild 101I-637-4192-23, Fotograf(in): Schalber)

Dams, waterways and marshalling yards

Beyond area bombing, there were two other ways the Ruhr industries could be disrupted. The first was attacking the region's dams. Before the war, an Air Targets Sub-Committee investigation had concluded that 3,000 sorties against the Möhne and Sorpe Dams would create the same amount of devastation as conventional area attacks on the Ruhr industries. At that time, British airmen were only too aware that larger bombs would be needed,[4] but a perceived vulnerability of the Ruhr industries to the destruction of the dams had been a longstanding Air Ministry perception.

The second target-set considered was the Ruhr's communications with the rest of Germany. These were essentially twofold: waterways and railways. On the former, the Air Targets Sub-Committee had also suggested the canal network leading to and from the Ruhr was especially vulnerable, especially those locks, aqueducts and embankments on the Dortmund–Ems and Mittelland waterways. In 1939–40, the canals were consistently viewed as potential targets for attack, with an initial inclination towards dropping 1,000lb bombs to sink barges, thereby creating obstructions. It was certainly felt that, however these inland waterways would be attacked, the Germans

4   See RAID 16 *Dambusters: Operation Chastise 1943*, by Douglas C. Dildy.

would be confronted with significant problems in the transportation of coal, coke and steel to other parts of the Reich, and the movement to the Ruhr of food and raw materials. Harris, famously unsympathetic to 'specialist' targets, did however recognize the Dortmund–Ems Canal was:

> the only link by water between the Ruhr and Eastern Germany or the North Sea and the Baltic; [in which] iron ore from Sweden inevitably goes through the canal to the Ruhr, and its barges carry millions of tons of freight to and from the Ruhr.

There were two other canals in the Ruhr: the Emscher Canal, which ran from Walsum to Dortmund, and the Rhine–Herne Canal, which connected the Rhine and the Dortmund–Ems and Mittelland canals. Inland harbours had made some Ruhr–Rhineland cities particularly important targets, with Europe's largest lying between Duisburg and Hamborn. The Ruhr also contained a huge network of railways – connecting its major towns, and the region, with the rest of Germany – around which had developed some huge marshalling yards.

However, certainly by Harris, transportation targets were considered to be useful collateral damage from area bombing rather than targets in their own right. Even where the Dortmund–Ems Canal

The tough, hardy, brave coal-miners of the Ruhr. They, together with their counterparts in the steelworks, factories, synthetic-oil plants, and on the railways, were considered legitimate targets of the British bombing campaign against the Ruhr's war economy. (Getty Images)

went over the River Ems via twin aqueducts – in an obvious 'bottleneck' near Münster – the aiming-point remained firmly over the city centre. A similar situation was found with Cologne, notwithstanding its major railway network and sizeable inland port. Yet intelligence reviewed by the MEW and Air Ministry stated that Bomber Command's attacks on the Ruhr cities had been very successful. By June, assessments were being made on how best Bomber Command could capitalize on the results of area bombing in the Ruhr. Studies convinced the Air Staff that attacks on the Ruhr's rail and waterborne communications would only serve to increase the chaos and dislocation. On 31 July – the final day of the Ruhr air campaign – HQ Bomber Command received a Directive ordering attacks on the inland waterways around the region. Little happened until 15–16 September, however, when 617 Squadron made an attempt on the embankments of the Dortmund–Ems Canal at Ladbergen (north-west of Münster), which ended in a costly fiasco. Later area attacks on Bochum (29–30 September) and Hagen (1–2 October) may also have been undertaken partly to disrupt railway communications in the central and southern Ruhr respectively; and also to fulfil the general aim of dislocating industrial production.

Synthetic oil plants

The Ruhr also contained ten synthetic oil plants – a consequence of the close proximity to major coalfields – and a number of Benzol plants owing to the large number of coking plants within the region. One town, Gelsenkirchen, had long held a fixation for the British Air Staff. It was a chief steam coal mining centre, a producer of steel and, most notably, the location for the two largest synthetic oil plants in the Reich, Gelsenkirchen-Nordstern and

Gelsenkirchen-Scholven, which occupied sites of 160 and 210 acres respectively. In April 1943, they were assessed to be producing 325,000 and 350,000 tons of oil per annum. Efforts at bombing Gelsenkirchen's oil plants in early 1941 soon disproved Bomber Command's belief that 200 sorties could knock a plant out for four months, and revealed in microcosm the considerable difficulty in locating cities, let alone particular installations. Harris, then Deputy Chief of the Air Staff, had been unimpressed, and he remained hostile towards these targets throughout his tenure as C-in-C Bomber Command. On 10 September 1942, in response to Bottomley's Directive to bomb synthetic oil plants, he responded:

> An attack on the two Gelsenkirchen Plants would be a waste of time and effort. They are both very small and difficult to find in the smoky and hazy atmosphere of the Ruhr. I do not believe that we have ever succeeded in damaging them and thousands of sorties have been wasted in the attempt. There is so much crying out to be done … that I am very much against this suggestion.

Despite some dispute over the low prioritization, raids against the Nordstern and Scholven synthetic oil plants would, during the Battle of the Ruhr, only happen within the context of the area bombing of Gelsenkirchen.

The Rhineland cities

In his post-war account, Harris listed Aachen, Cologne, Düsseldorf, Krefeld, Mönchengladbach and Münster as having been attacked during the Battle of the Ruhr. These towns, as he acknowledged, were 'not, of course, strictly within the Ruhr area, but belonged to the same industrial complex'. One of the most important, some 20 miles south-west of Essen, was Düsseldorf, which had a population of about 530,000. Described as being 'just as important as Essen', but easier to identify because it lay on the Rhine, Düsseldorf was most famous for the giant Rheinmetall-Borsig Works, a 1+ priority target, which owing to pre-war expansion was considered the equal of Krupps. Other important factories included the Mannesmannröhren Werke and the plants of J.G. Schwietzke. These firms meant Düsseldorf was a centre of armaments production – making flak guns, bombs, shells, mines and torpedoes – and the machine tool industry ('without an adequate supply of these no factory can carry on', one Air Ministry Bulletin noted). The city also possessed the giant Darendorf marshalling yard and the third largest inland port in Germany. The MEW emphasized Düsseldorf's pivotal role as the administrative capital of most iron and steel producers, heavy engineering industries and armaments plants of the Ruhr–Rhineland area, and the 'destruction of these head offices and of the records in them would cause a lot of muddle and loss of production' (post-war evidence from Reich Minister for Armaments and War Production, Albert Speer, suggested this was not the case). It was no surprise that even before March 1943, Düsseldorf had been a regular target for Bomber Command: Harris sent a large force of 630 aircraft, including OTU (Operational Training Unit) crews, to bomb the city in bright moonlight and clear weather on 31 July–1 August 1942, and made a further attack on 10–11 September with a

Tank production at the other major centre of German arms production, Rheinmetall-Borsig in Düsseldorf. Here workers are being addressed by the commander-in-chief of the German army, Colonel-General Walther von Brauchitsch, before the war began. (Getty Images)

Main Force of 479 bombers now led by the Pathfinders. These two attacks, Harris wrote, 'caused very extensive damage in the centre of the city, and profitable damage was inflicted in a number of industrial plants and railway facilities', a clear sign that, at this time, damage to factories and transportation was perceived, in modern terminology, as 'useful collateral' of the area bombing of a city centre. During the Battle of the Ruhr, the goal was the destruction of Düsseldorf's reconstructed factories, which, notwithstanding a shortage of labour and building materials, had been laboriously rebuilt over the previous six months.

BELOW
Rhine coal barges transporting the Ruhr's rich coal deposits to factories throughout Germany. (Getty Images)

RHINELAND CITIES & TOWNS

Target (codename)	Approx pop size	Description of importance	Total Key-Point Rating (KPR)
Aachen (Elver)	164,000	Textiles, Tyres, Electrical Engineering, Glass, Transportation	20
Cologne (Trout)	906,000	Light Engineering, U-Boat Diesel Engines, U-Boat Batteries, Chemicals, Synthetic Oil, Artificial Rubber, Explosives, Textiles, Transportation Humboldt-Deutz (Priority 1+) Gottfried Hagen (Priority 1) Wesseling synthetic-oil plant (250,000 p.a.) Köln Nippes M/Y (7,500) Kalk Nord M/Y (5,600) Gereon M/Y (3,200) Riverside docks	126
Düsseldorf (Perch)	541,000	Armaments, Machine Tools, Steel Tubing, Plastics, Transportation Rheinmetall-Borsig Works (Priority 1+) Mannesmannröhren Werke (Priority 1) J.G. Schwietzke (Priority 3) Düsseldorf-Darendorf M/Y (2,100) Inland port area	158
Hamm	56,000	Transportation Hamm M/Y (10,000)	
Leverkusen (Bluefin)	50,000	Chemicals, Vehicles IG Farben (Priority 1) Ford Works (Priority 3)	
Mönchengladbach/ Rheydt (Jack)	205,000	Textile production	12
Münster (Rudd)	141,000	Transportation Münster M/Y Dortmund–Ems canal	16

Southwards from Düsseldorf, along the River Rhine, lay Germany's third largest city, Cologne. Representing something of an obsession for Harris, this foremost centre of transportation in the Rhineland saw goods from the Ruhr cities pass through on their way to either southern or western Germany, or beyond to Western Europe, either by Rhine barge or rail. Cologne thus became the chief railway centre of the Rhineland, a junction for railway lines from the Ruhr, southern Germany, the Low Countries and Paris. Famously bombed in the first 'Thousand-Bomber' operation in mid-1942 and later subjected to heavy attacks in late 1944, in between Cologne would not be

OPPOSITE TARGETS BEYOND THE RUHR: TACTICAL 'DIVERSIONS' AND OTHER CENTRES OF WAR PRODUCTION

As observed in the *British Official History*, 'though the Battle did have a geographical heart in the Ruhr itself, it is interesting to note that of the first ten major attacks on German targets after the initial thrust against Essen on 5th March only four were against towns in the Ruhr valley'. This was partly because of the weather cancelling Ruhr operations, partly because of the tactical need to bomb targets away from the Ruhr/Rhineland area and partly because of a need to destroy other industrial targets considered vital to the Axis war economy. The latter saw attacks on the Skoda Works at Pilsen (German-occupied Czechoslovakia), the Schneider Works at Le Creusot (France) – which Secretary of State for Air Sir Archibald Sinclair described as 'one of the great armaments factories of the world' – and Fiat's numerous factories in Turin. There were also attacks on Stuttgart (codename: Barbel), the great industrial centre of southern Germany, which contained the Daimler-Benz factory and the Robert Bosch Works, producing aero-engines, tank powerplants and electrical components, respectively. Bombing a target such as Stuttgart was thus made in the wake of attacking Krupps of Essen and the Skoda Works in Pilsen. In addition, bombing the Ruhr required British bombers to cross the Kammhuber Line whose plotting stations relied on specially produced components made at the Zeiss optical instruments factory in Jena. Similarly, the Zeppelin Works at Friedrichshafen, on the Swiss–German border, produced the Würzburg radars. At sea, this period saw extensive minelaying operations of the sea lanes through the Kattegat, Danish Belts and Baltic to Germany, together with the mining of the Kiel Canal, the coastal waters in Kiel Bay, the Elbe Estuary and Danzig Bay, all designed to sink the shipping carrying iron ore from Sweden to the war industries of the Ruhr. This trade was considerable with 7.5 million tons being transported from Swedish ports and 1.6 million tons coming through Narvik in 1942 alone. In addition, Norway exported molybdenum extracted from the mines at Knaben, destined for the steelworks of Bochum where it was used for producing special chromium molybdenum steels. Interdicting these supplies was therefore a priority. Harris later wrote that Germany's merchant fleet was 'the main target for our mines'. 'Particular attention,' he continued, 'was paid to the traffic in iron ore from Scandinavia to the Ruhr [precisely because] the denial of raw material supplies by dislocation and sinking would be complementary to the bombing effort then being directed against the industries of the Ruhr.' 2 Group also made daylight attacks on merchant vessels docked in the Channel ports and bombed Rotterdam's docks on 29 March and 4 April. The other aspect of Bomber Command's non-Ruhr operations was to prevent the concentration of Germany's air defences solely in and around that region. To be sure, some targets had additional reasons for being attacked, such as worsening German morale during a time of major setbacks on the Eastern Front by bombing Berlin (Operation *Tannenburg*), or attacking cities that were symbolically important for the Nazi movement, namely Nuremberg and Munich. Attacking these targets, together with places such as Frankfurt, Mannheim and Stuttgart, forced the Germans to keep the flak and night-fighter defences strong throughout most parts of the Reich. Bomber Command's Mosquitoes were very active in this regard, with those of 2 Group (soon transferred to the PFF) undertaking 'diversionary' raids on Berlin. Mosquitoes also conducted operations against Ruhr targets on nights when the Main Force was not operating, either to recalibrate and test Oboe or to wear down the morale of the German population by keeping the air-raid sirens blazing.

spared either, being bombed four times during the Battle of the Ruhr. Industrially, Cologne specialized in light engineering, chemicals and synthetic oil production, artificial rubber, explosives and textiles. War production expanded considerably from 1939, with the older industrial areas in the city and the districts of Nippes, Knapsack and Brauweiler joined by factories established along the Rhine's right bank in Kalk and Deutz; these areas, together with Mülheim, formed a compact area of five square miles densely packed with industries, railway lines and workers (170,000 people lived here out of Cologne's total population of 906,000). The Deutz area contained the Humboldt-Deutz factory, which made diesel engines for U-boats, and the Gottfried Hagen plant, that produced accumulator batteries for these vessels. A factory in the Ruhr–Rhineland could thus have critical importance for another element of Germany's war production.

The Rhineland's smaller cities comprised Aachen, situated near the Dutch border; the textile production centre of Mönchengladbach-Rheydt; and Münster, an important junction for rail and canal transportation leading to and from the Ruhr. The other notable town was Leverkusen, home of an IG Farben chemical plant and a Ford Works, which would not be attacked during the Battle of the Ruhr but would be targeted in August and November 1943.

North Sea

Baltic Sea

SWEDEN

DENMARK

GERMANY

NETHERLANDS

BELGIUM

UNITED KINGDOM

FRANCE

SWITZERLAND

ITALY

English Channel

Bay of Biscay

■ Minelaying areas

N

100 miles
100 km
0

Minelaying:
27/28 April; 28/29 April; 21/22 May
Kiel Bay, northern German coast, Brittany, Frisian
Islands, Texel, Heligoland, Elbe estuary, Danish
Belts, Biscay Ports, River Gironde, La Pallice
Economic: mining sea-lanes in which supplies
came into German occupied Europe, including
Swedish iron ore (many minelaying operations
were undertaken but these were the largest)
Strategic: helping the war at sea against
Germany's U-boats and surface fleet

Hamburg
24/25 July
Tactical: first nuisance raid by Mosquitoes designed to confuse
German air defences and prevent concentration near Ruhr
Strategic: beginning of Battle of Hamburg overlaps with end
of Ruhr campaign

Wilhelmshaven
13/14 April
Tactical: first nuisance raid by Mosquitoes designed to confuse
German air defences and prevent concentration near Ruhr

Ijmuiden
2 May
Economic: attack on steelworks by 2 Group's
Bostons and Venturas in daylight

Rotterdam
29 March
Economic: major docks attacked
by 2 Group's Venturas in daylight

Lorient
2/3 April
Strategic: assist the Battle of the
Atlantic by bombing U-boat pens

St. Nazaire
22/23 March; 28/29 March; 2/3 April
Strategic: assist the Battle of the Atlantic
by bombing U-boat pens

Kiel
4/5 April
Economic: bombing the docks that
received iron ore from Sweden

Rostock
20/21 April
Economic: Heinkel aircraft factory

Stettin
20/21 April
Economic: bombing docks receiving Swedish iron ore
by bombing major supply port for
German forces on the Eastern Front
Tactical: stretching Germany's air defences away from the Ruhr

Berlin
27/28 March; 29/30 March
Political: capital of the Third Reich
Tactical: stretching Germany's air defences away from the Ruhr

Bremen
13/14 April
Tactical: first nuisance raid by Mosquitoes designed to confuse
German air defences and prevent concentration near Ruhr

Frankfurt
10/11 April
Economic: Major industrial centre
Tactical: stretching Germany's air
defences away from the Ruhr

Jena
27 May
Economic: attack on Zeiss optical instruments
factory by 2 Group's Mosquitoes in daylight

Pilsen
16/17 April; 13/14 May
Economic: Skoda armament works

Nuremberg
8/9 March
Political: city of symbolic importance to Nazi movement
Tactical: stretching Germany's air defences away from the Ruhr

Munich
9/10 March
Political: city of symbolic importance to Nazi movement
Tactical: stretching Germany's air defences away from the Ruhr

Mannheim
16/17 April
Economic: Major industrial centre
Tactical: stretching Germany's air defences away from the Ruhr

Stuttgart
11/12 March; 14/15 April
Economic: major industrial centre
Tactical: stretching Germany's air defences away from the Ruhr

Montbeliard
15/16 July
Economic: Peugeot Works

Le Creusot
19/20 June
Economic: major centre of French
armaments production (Schneider Works)

Friedrichshafen
20/21 June
Tactical: attack on Zeppelin Works making Würzburg radars for Kammhuber line
Strategic: assist Mediterranean war by attacking major naval base of the Italian battlefleet
Tactical: stretching Germany's air defences away from the Ruhr and from North Africa

La Spezia
13/14 April; 19/19 April; 23/24 June ('shuttle attack' to North Africa)
Strategic: assist Mediterranean war by attacking major naval base of the Italian battlefleet
Tactical: stretching Germany's air defences away from the Ruhr

Turin
12/13 July
Economic: major centre of Italian war production (Fiat Works)
Strategic: assist Mediterranean war during Sicily invasion
Tactical: stretching Germany's air defences away from the Ruhr

• Kiel
• Rostock
• Hamburg
• Stettin
• Berlin
• Bremen
• Wilhelmshaven
• Ijmuiden
• Rotterdam
• Frankfurt
• Jena
• Pilsen
• Mannheim
• Nuremberg
• Stuttgart
• Munich
• Friedrichshafen
• Montbeliard
• Le Creusot
• Turin
• La Spezia
• Lorient
• St. Nazaire

THE CAMPAIGN
The bomber battle in 'Happy Valley'

A crashed Halifax II from 76 Squadron at Holme-on-Spalding. The aircraft had suffered considerable damage on the Essen operation of 25–26 July when the propeller flew off and sliced into the fuselage. (© IWM CE 91)

Precursor: the 'experimental' Ruhr attacks and 'diversions', December 1942–February 1943

Throughout winter 1942–43, Bomber Command was in a period of technical and tactical development, which saw the first operational testing of Oboe on 20–21 December 1942, the Oboe sky-marking technique (Musical Wanganui) on 31 December 1942–1 January 1943, the coloured target-indicator bomb (TI) on 16–17 January, the Oboe ground-marking technique (Musical Parramatta)[5] on 27–28 January and the performance of H2S on 30–31 January. Apart from Oboe, which was first tested by six Mosquitoes from 109 Squadron who used it to bomb Lutterade Power Station in Holland, and the TI, which was first tested on Berlin, these 'experimental' attacks were all undertaken against the Ruhr in different conditions and against a number of different targets. Starting with Düsseldorf on 31 December 1942–1 January 1943, but including Essen and specific areas of Duisburg, with just Mosquitoes, the attacks became larger as small numbers of Lancasters became involved. Further Lancasters from one and then two Bomber Groups joined the attacks, and finally mixed forces of different aircraft types. In addition, the Main Force was now being assisted by the PFF, designated 8 Group, with not just navigation but the actual marking of the aiming-point. Consequently, this was a progressively increasing testing programme that was designed to get Bomber Command ready for opening its main offensive against Germany.

It was vital to determine how far Oboe assisted the accurate dropping of sky-markers, for the Ruhr, either because of thick cloud or dense industrial ground-haze, was often attacked in conditions when ground detail could simply not be seen. As the campaign went on, Bomber Command's increasing losses often forced it to operate against the Ruhr in cloudy conditions

5 If Oboe was used to assist a Parramatta or Wanganui attack, then the word 'Musical' preceded either of these terms.

so the British aircraft would have some protection from the heavy air defences. After the 8–9 January attack on Duisburg, enough visual evidence was acquired to show sky-marking could deliver a reasonable degree of accuracy, if not a really heavy bombing concentration around the aiming-point. Similarly, a few photographs had shown the 'experimental' sky-marker raids had caused damage throughout Essen and the Krupp Works: a considerable achievement given the difficulties of bombing this target back in 1942. This was enough evidence to convince the research section 'boffins' at HQ Bomber Command that Oboe had a theoretical accuracy rate of 650 yards. However, the perennial weakness of sky-markers was their tendency to drift in the wind, which meant the bombers' precise arrival timings were absolutely critical. Yet the real cause for optimism was that 60 per cent of the force had bombed within three miles of Essen; in all previous attacks on this target, this figure had been as low as 20 per cent. This meant that a sufficient bomber force could bludgeon large areas, if not specific targets, and HQ Bomber Command was pleased by the overall results, confident that Oboe at last unlocked the formula for making accurate – or at least reasonably accurate – attacks on the Ruhr. Oboe's ability to allow bombing on sky-markers, as Harris wrote later, 'did prevent the total failure of an operation and certainly produced enough damage to be worth while'.

With Düsseldorf having been the object of the first Oboe sky-marking attack, that same city was used for the first Oboe-led ground-marking attack on 27–28 January. For the first time, Harris sent the Mosquito markers at the head of a large force of 157 heavy bombers, which were tightly concentrated so the entire raid lasted no longer than 20 minutes. Three Mosquitoes from 109 Squadron dropped their red primary markers, whilst 13 Lancaster 'backers-up' visually identified the aiming-point and dropped their secondary markers, which were green; the old method of simply illuminating the target through dropping masses of white flares was now clearly discarded. During this period of experimentation, coloured target-indicators had first been used operationally on Berlin, but it was an unhappy debut, with poor conditions and against a target well beyond Oboe range. Nonetheless, the intention remained for marrying these new TIs with Oboe, and in what would become the standard procedure for a ground-marking attack during the Battle of the Ruhr, the Main Force was told to aim at the red TIs. If not seen, then the best concentration of green secondary markers was to be bombed instead. On 27–28 January, in 10–10 or total low cloud cover, the glowing TIs were still seen by the Main Force, whose bombing was successfully concentrated in southern Düsseldorf. Thus, by early February, three marking techniques had been developed: Newhaven for a target seen visually in below 5–10 cloud cover; Parramatta for ground-marking in 5–8–10 cloud (considered 'blind ground-marking); and Wanganui in conditions above 8–10 cloud in which sky-markers would be required. In all these methods, both Oboe or H2S could be used. H2S was tested extensively as a target-marking device at this time, starting with operations against Germany's ports of Hamburg and Wilhelmshaven in January and February, coastal targets in which the sharp contrast between the sea and land could be highlighted. But it was Oboe, installed in the high-flying Mosquitoes, which could be flown much more steadily over the target because of being largely invulnerable to night fighters and flak, that would be preferred for bombing the Ruhr.

By February 1943, Bomber Command had its new marking TI devices, accompanying techniques for marking in visual and blind conditions, and growing front-line strength in heavy bombers. This 'technical revolution', in the official historians' words, meant

Harris visits a bomber station on 10 May 1943, and watches a Halifax undergo considerable maintenance, including two engine changes. Keeping the bombers flying was a huge challenge for the maintenance crews. (Getty Images)

Harris' force had 'as far as finding and hitting the target was concerned, the basic devices upon which the new tactics of the strategic air offensive were founded'. Ready as it was, it might be wondered as to why the Battle of the Ruhr was not launched four weeks sooner. The delay was certainly not a consequence of the weather. Wintry but clear weather meant February 1943 proved a busy month for Bomber Command. Out of 28 nights, Harris sent the Main Force out 16 times, but, notwithstanding bombing Cologne three times, no targets in the Ruhr–Rhineland were attacked. This was because of Harris' orders. Aware that the Casablanca Directive's primary aim of 'the progressive destruction and dislocation of the German military, industrial and economic system and undermining the morale of the German people' did, broadly speaking, permit the Battle of the Ruhr, the Directive's specific tasks were U-boat construction yards, the German aircraft industry, transportation facilities, 'other targets in [the] enemy war industry' and 'on demand' objectives (northern Italy and Berlin).

Formally receiving this Directive on 4 February, Harris no doubt felt it was better to secure some goodwill by bombing these targets before commencing the Battle of the Ruhr. Thus, a particular concentration was made on Wilhelmshaven, but Berlin and Nuremberg – important political targets whose bombing Churchill desired to impress the Soviets – were also attacked several times during this period. So too were the major industrial centres of northern Italy, Turin and Milan, which had been formally requested on 17 January. However, the most intense effort, and in Harris' eyes the most odious, was the Air Ministry's demand for bombing the U-boat bases in the Biscay ports: Lorient, St. Nazaire, Brest and La Pallice. Twelve major attacks between 14 January and 6 April delayed the start of the Ruhr campaign by two months, although this delay allowed the Oboe Mosquitoes to gain more experience of the primary-marking role. As this bombing offensive was intended to last a year, 'the loss of two months', Harris later complained, 'which may have seemed a small affair to the authorities at the time, may now be seen in its proper perspective'. Though Harris was overstating the supposed decisive effects of attacking German cities during 1943–44, nonetheless it meant the campaign's final stages, as will be seen, stretched into the summer, with light nights and all the consequent effects on operations and rising casualties. Thus, right on the eve of commencing the Battle of the Ruhr, Harris was submitting a formal protest on the issue of 'diversions' of his bombers to a multitude of targets, some well away from Germany. In a letter dated 6 March, he complained at the number of Directives (amounting to 17) that had been sent by the Air Ministry since 19 November 1942, which revealed 'the absence of any continuity of plan for the prosecution of the Bomber Offensive against Germany'.

The main battle begins: Essen and Duisburg, March–April

Given the longstanding RAF obsession with the Krupp Works, rather predictably Essen was the chief focus of the battle's opening period. Given its location in a heavily defended area, the fact that it was often shrouded by an industrial haze and was not readily distinguishable from surrounding urban areas such as Oberhausen (especially if bomb-aimers were blinded by the numerous searchlights), Essen seemed an unpromising place to begin an air campaign. Yet it was precisely this sort of target, with these sorts of obstacles, that Oboe had been designed and tested to overcome. Moreover, starting with Essen actually possessed some advantages. On one level, Krupps was well-known, and hitting this military-industrial target would earn Bomber Command some plaudits, both domestically and internationally. More significantly, the sheer size of the Krupps site meant it formed a considerable proportion of the town of Essen itself; in other words, both town and factory could perish at the same time. This made Essen unique. Far more commonplace in Germany was the city in which a giant factory lay in the suburbs, 'where', Harris stated, 'they could not easily be destroyed in the course of area attack'; the huge armament works of Rheinmetall-Borsig in Düsseldorf's southern suburbs was a prime example. Apart from Essen, aiming-points for other German cities therefore comprised the city centres, which often had large populations packed into or near an *Altstadt* full of timbered buildings ripe for concentrated attack by incendiary bombs. Physical damage to surrounding factories came from the inaccuracies of area bombing itself, but generally the objective was to reduce production in the factories more by 'indirect damage' to housing, local transportation and public utilities than 'by any direct damage' to industrial sites themselves.

So it was that Essen was attacked on 5–6 March, and the target-marking technique of the campaign's opening attack was Oboe-led blind ground-marking (Musical Parramatta). Designed to mark the Krupp Works accurately – and to bring about its, and Essen's, destruction – the operation plan saw three successive waves with a total of 442 British bombers organized to maximize the impact of the attack. The first wave comprised all the Halifaxes, which were to drop a good proportion of high-explosives and incendiaries to break roofs and start fires; the second wave contained the Wellingtons and Stirlings, whose considerable loads were designed to intensify the existing conflagrations, before the all-Lancaster final wave added their large HE loads to provide a violent end and keep Essen's firefighters away from tackling the fires taking hold. This plan certainly worked, and Essen was engulfed by a seemingly solid circle of fires two miles in diameter, in which smoke rose to 15,000ft, and whose glow could be seen for 150 miles on the bombers' return journey. There were numerous large explosions, with one some 20 minutes into the attack leaving a huge orange cloud hanging in the sky for several minutes afterwards that served to illuminate the nearby streets. As the *British Official History* describes the opening attack, it 'was, if not an unqualified, at least an unprecedented, success'. The Reich's Minister for Propaganda, Joseph Goebbels – someone whose entire public career was based on distortion and half-truths – often wrote in his diary frank descriptions of the results of British bombing raids. Following this attack, he noted that Essen had suffered 'an exceptionally severe raid', with the Krupp Works particularly 'hard hit' and a 'considerable' number of dead. Moreover, Goebbels perceived the impact of such attacks on civilian morale. 'If the English continue their raids on this scale', he continued:

they will make things exceedingly difficult for us. The dangerous things about this matter, looking at it psychologically, is that the population can see no way of [us] doing anything about it. Our anti-aircraft guns are inadequate. The successes of our night fighters, though notable, are not sufficient to compel the English to desist from their night attacks.

However, the weather could compel Bomber Command to desist. Harris was set to send his bombers back to Essen the following night, but this was cancelled 30 minutes before take-off owing to poor weather over the bases, much to the relief of Flight Lieutenant Don Charlwood, a navigator in 103 Squadron based at Elsham Wolds in Lincolnshire. Charlwood and crew (and many others) thereafter boarded a bus for the pubs of Scunthorpe. Over the next nights, no operations to the Ruhr were undertaken, with Harris instead preferring long-distance trips to Nuremberg, Munich and Stuttgart for tactical reasons (see below), before attacking Essen again on 12–13 March. The techniques and methods of the previous attack were repeated, and this time left a vast rectangular inferno. British aircrews reported that fires 'gained a good hold and merged into huge masses of red flames', which may have indicated a 'firestorm' was taking place, and a huge explosion at 2245hrs, nearly an hour after the attack had finished, caused a vast white flash seen by aircraft over the Dutch coast. The British bomber crews had pressed home their attack in the face of very determined opposition, for the Germans, quickly ascertaining the direction from which the bombers had arrived over Essen on the previous raid, had accordingly strengthened their ground defences north of the Ruhr. A searchlight belt comprising large cones of 50 or 60 searchlights and smaller cones of about 20 beams was now positioned about 4½ miles from Essen, probably in the towns of Bottrop, Gladbeck and Scholven, which formed an arc from the north-west to the north-east.

EVENTS

1   2045hrs. Eight Oboe Mosquitos leaving at set times lead the attack, flying on a separate course to the other bomber forces; they approach Essen from the direction of Oberhausen.

2   2045hrs. The other bomber forces approach Essen from the north with the Main Force flying in three waves. The first section comprises the Halifaxes of 4 and 6 Groups; the second section contains 3 Group's Stirlings and all the Wellingtons (from various Groups); and the third section the Lancasters of 1 and 5 Groups. 22 PFF Lancasters also fly with the Main Force at two-minute intervals, and these aircraft drop yellow flares 15 miles north of the target to assist navigation. They will also be backers-up for the Oboe Mosquitos throughout the duration of the raid. In total, 442 aircraft have been sent on the opening attack in the Battle of the Ruhr, although only 367 attack the primary target.

3   2100hrs. Zero Hour over Essen. PFF Mosquitoes and Lancasters backers-up commence marking the target (method: Oboe groundmarking); all PFF aircraft are allotted set times e.g. 2nd Mosquito at zero + 5, 3rd Mosquito at zero + 10, 4th Mosquito at zero + 13, etc. The Mosquitoes, using Oboe, mark the aiming-point over the Krupp Works with salvoes of red TIs. The 22 Lancaster backers-up attack at one to two minute intervals from between zero + 2 and zero + 38, aiming green TIs and

HE in salvoes at the red TIs. This method means the aiming-point remains marked throughout the attack, with a clearly distinguishable point seen by all crews, vital given Essen's notorious industrial haze that made visual identification often impossible. Main Force aircraft are instructed to only bomb on the coloured TIs, and if arriving early they are to turn left and perform a circuit around the Essen area until these can be seen.

4   2102–2120hrs. Main Force Section 1 (Halifaxes) commences bombing.

5   2115–2125hrs. Main Force Section 2 (Stirlings and Wellingtons) commences bombing.

6   2120–2140hrs. Main Force Section 3 (Lancasters) commences bombing.

7   2058–2138hrs. Moderate to intense predicted heavy flak fired up to 20,000ft. Many searchlights co-operate in cones; the flak is particularly accurate against 'seen' targets. As the attack develops, searchlights' control lessens and flak is fired in barrage form. British tactics of concentrating the bomber force saturates and dislocates the searchlight and flak defences helping to minimize losses to anti-aircraft fire. The attack is completed in 28 minutes. Only 14 bombers (3.2%) are lost, seven due to Essen's flak and the others to night fighters along the routes. This is a low casualty rate for a notorious target.

G

Oberhausen

Duisburg-Ruhrort inland port

Duisburg

River Rhine

10

The opening attack: Essen, 5–6 March 1943

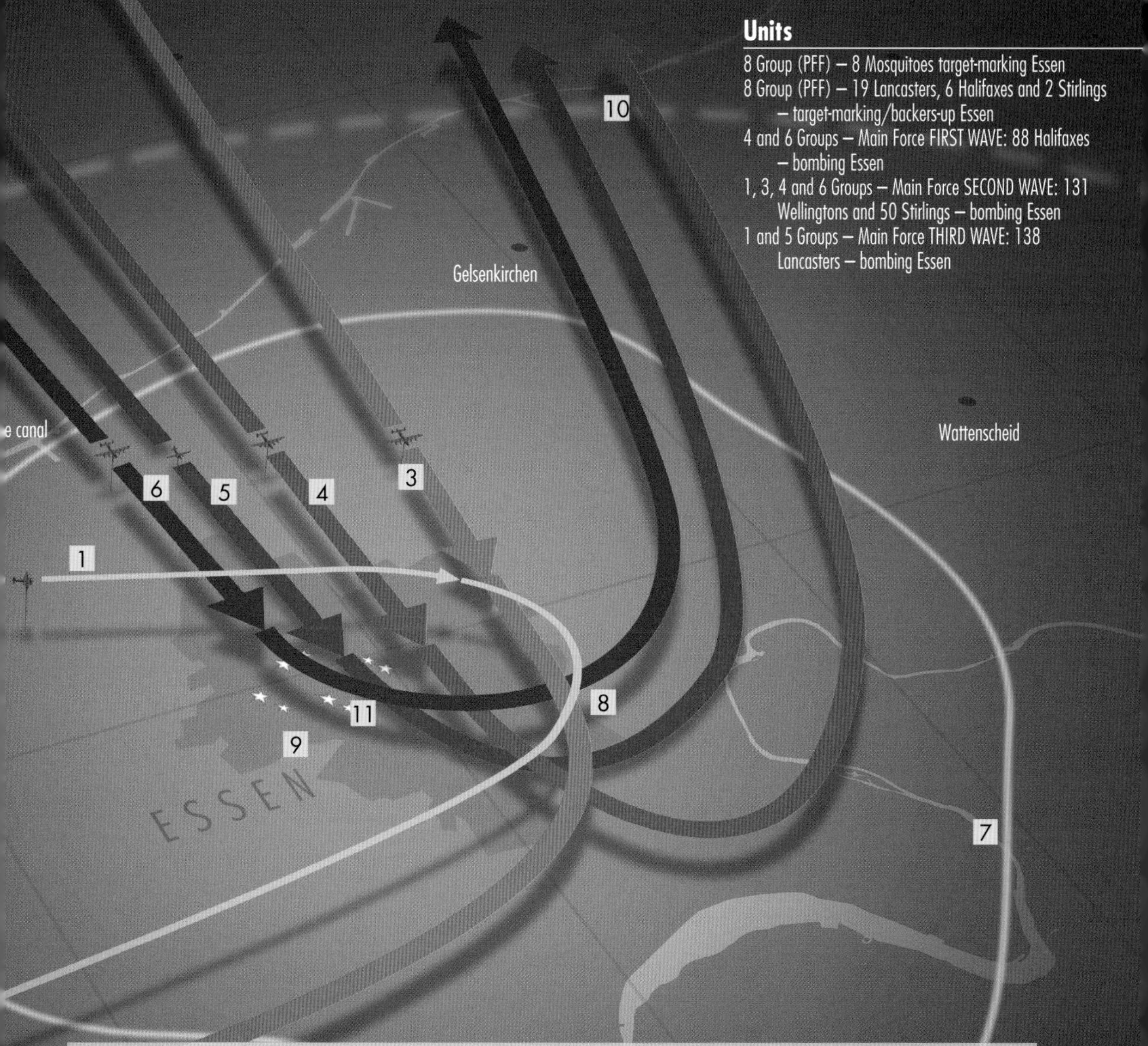

Units

8 Group (PFF) – 8 Mosquitoes target-marking Essen
8 Group (PFF) – 19 Lancasters, 6 Halifaxes and 2 Stirlings
 – target-marking/backers-up Essen
4 and 6 Groups – Main Force FIRST WAVE: 88 Halifaxes
 – bombing Essen
1, 3, 4 and 6 Groups – Main Force SECOND WAVE: 131
 Wellingtons and 50 Stirlings – bombing Essen
1 and 5 Groups – Main Force THIRD WAVE: 138
 Lancasters – bombing Essen

Gelsenkirchen

Wattenscheid

e canal

ESSEN

er Ruhr

EVENTS

8 2102–2138hrs. British bomber crews see several German fighters around the target area, but few combats take place. The fighters seemed to be being used for flak and searchlights to confirm the height and track of individual bombers. British interception of German wireless traffic ascertains there are nine ground-controlled patrols, with 11 pursuits but only one combat. Considerable interference is made by the British using Tinsel to jam German radio transmissions.

9 2100–2138hrs. With the red and green target indicators having been dropped accurately around the Krupp Works aiming-point, Main Force's bombing is very concentrated. Fires take hold in the target area and soon become a two-mile largely uninterrupted radius around the aiming-point. A huge explosion happens at 21.07hrs and is followed by another two at 21.20hrs.

10 2150hrs. British bombers are now well clear of the Essen area, leaving behind a blazing target. All PFF aircraft leave westwards heading towards Rheinhausen, whilst all Main Force aircraft, having performed a sharp left turn after bombing the target, travel northwards in the direction of Recklinghausen. Both forces head towards the Dutch coast at different points on their way back to the UK.

11 Day reconnaissance sorties flown on 7 and 8 March report that the 'destruction was shown to be exceptionally severe and widespread, the heaviest concentration being in the town centre, which was virtually devastated; an area of over 160 acres was laid waste. It is estimated that in the town proper and its environs, there are approximately 450 acres where at least 75% of the buildings were demolished or gutted by fire … By far the greater part of the damage appears to have resulted from fire'. The Krupp Works has 53 machining shops and 13 main buildings destroyed or damaged.

The Ruhr's railways, leading eastward, congregated at Hamm, which contained huge marshalling yards. Perhaps Germany's equivalent of the British railway town and junction of Crewe, Hamm had been a target for Bomber Command in 1940–41 when German communications had been a priority target for the British. In the Battle of the Ruhr, Hamm would be untouched and, in fact, was not bombed again by Bomber Command until 5 December 1944. The US Eighth did undertake three modest attacks on the town's marshalling yards in February and March 1943, however. (© IWM C 1768)

Smoke generators had been added to emit clouds to cover the towns and factories, and so too were more flak guns, which provided a noticeably heavier barrage than before. Some of the latter were railway-mounted flak guns quickly despatched to the area, whose noise would at least hearten the local population into believing that a vigorous defence was taking place. Yet the British bombers still got through, and both attacks brought Bomber Command, and Harris in particular, a considerable amount of praise from Portal. The Chief of the Air Staff, enthused by the reports and photographs from 7 March, wrote to Harris six days later to say the results against the Krupp Works were magnificent. To the C-in-C, his strategy of using area bombing to break industrial Germany was seemingly being vindicated.

Harris was only too keen to circulate the efforts of Bomber Command, sensing the results were useful on the other side of the Atlantic. On 25 March, he sent photographs of a damaged Essen to the American assistant secretary of war for air, Robert Lovatt, no doubt to show the striking power of Bomber Command and to get the American effort much more mobilized on bombing Germany; it was, after all, a combined bombing offensive. 'I emphasize', he told the American, 'that the effects of our campaign would be vastly greater if the U.S.A.A.F. had sufficient aircraft here to enable them to operate over Germany in substantial numbers in daylight', which would contribute to 'wearing down' the Luftwaffe and the flak defences. Certainly on the British side, there was growing concern – and scepticism – about the American effort against Germany, which remained small and sporadic. By late June and well into the Ruhr air campaign, the tonnage of bombs dropped by Bomber Command was seven-and-a-half times larger than that released by the US Eighth Air Force. But targets in Germany's industrial heartland were ones the Americans were keen to avoid in spring 1943, which was wise – inexperienced American crews really could not be sent deep into the Ruhr at this time in daylight. Hamm was on the Ruhr's outer, eastern fringes. Yet it only seems fair to mention that on 4 March, the US Eighth had attacked an important transportation target near the Ruhr: Hamm and its huge marshalling yards. Reconnaissance photographs showed the American bombing was impressively accurate, with the modest number of aircraft having inflicted severe damage on the platforms, buildings and tracks around the main railway station. Harris would not attack Hamm during this campaign; after all, it was a transportation target, not an industrial city.

Instead, Bomber Command continued to attack Essen, mounting its third operation on 3–4 April. Although an uncertain weather forecast had seen the PFF prepare for a Musical Wanganui attack by taking sky-markers in case cloud covered the target, in the end the Oboe blind ground-marking technique was used. The German defences of decoy sites and the violent flak barrage did little to stop the bombers from hitting the Krupp Works again – the third attack on the 800-acre site, showing just how vast this was. Within days, Goebbels arrived to see for himself the level of Essen's destruction. Met at the main railway station, the Nazi entourage was soon forced to complete the journey to the hotel on foot because the rubble-strewn streets had made driving impossible. 'This walk', Goebbels wrote on 10 April, allowed 'a first-hand estimate of the damage inflicted by the last three raids', and was:

colossal and indeed ghastly. This city must, for the most part, be written off completely. The city's building experts estimate that it will take twelve years to repair the damage … Nobody can tell how Krupps can go on.

But with some degree of foresight, Goebbels was against the dispersal of Krupps from Essen, because once 'the English' had ascertained the city was no longer a functioning industrial centre, he feared they would simply move on to 'the next city', be it Bochum, Dortmund or Düsseldorf. This lends credence to the view of some later historians who argued that from spring 1943, the Krupp Works had limited industrial activity, and in effect became one giant decoy site that continued to exercise a magnetic attraction for Bomber Command right to the war's end. Certainly its sheer size always convinced the British that, although damage had been done, industrial activity in some part of the Krupp Works was continuing and hence needed repeat bombing. The Air Ministry's Bulletin after the next attack, on 30 April–1 May, even stated that 'the works are so extensive that they still offer a number of targets'.

Thus, for the fourth time in six weeks, Harris sent his bombers to Essen which saw the force of 305 aircraft battle bitterly cold conditions of -28C and thick icy clouds up to 20,000ft, as well as the German defenders. Unlike the previous efforts utilizing Oboe ground-marking, the 10/10 cloud meant the Musical Wanganui method had to be used. The target remained covered, but the clear visibility above the cloud meant the PFF's sky-markers could be seen, and certainly bombs were falling around Essen. But Bomber Command HQ was only too aware that this marking method meant concentrated levels of bombing and destruction were unlikely. British post-raid analysis was hampered by the thick cloud preventing night photographs from being taken, yet German reports stated that bombs had fallen throughout Essen, around the Krupp Works and in ten other Ruhr towns, especially Bottrop. Nonetheless, although a concentrated level of bombing was always preferable, indeed vital, for Bomber Command's heavy destruction of a target, scattered bombing in the Ruhr in poor weather conditions was better than not operating at all. Indeed, reconnaissance photographs of the western Ruhr area – which showed minor damage in Duisburg, Hamborn, Oberhausen, Mülheim, Bochum and Bottrop – saw Harris scribble on the Interpretation Report dated 17 April, 'useful incidental damage by shorts & overs'. On the German side, it has often been forgotten that poor weather hindered their efforts too; on this occasion the searchlights could not penetrate through the thick cloud, and the hundreds of heavy flak guns instead fired in an intense barrage up to 23,000ft.

A British reconnaissance photograph (left) taken in December 1939, which the Air Ministry labelled as the 'dark Satanic mills' of Krupps at Essen and representative of 'a black country if ever there was one'. The contrast with the damaged Krupp Works in March 1943 (right) was striking. (© IWM C 2353 and C 3457)

Overall, Bomber Command's significant effort in these first three attacks had severely damaged about 600 acres of Essen's built-up area, with some 250 acres being in the Krupp Works itself; nearly 4,000 workers' homes were also destroyed. The last attack, as mentioned, added scattered damage throughout Essen and the numerous towns surrounding it. Principally, a high level of general destruction had been achieved, but whether this had been enough to knock out the city and its giant industrial concern was open to question. Certainly, Harris felt compelled to revisit Essen twice more during the Battle of the Ruhr, the final attack on 25–26 July comprising a vast force of 705 aircraft.

The other target attacked during the campaign's opening two months was the great inland port and industrial centre of Duisburg, which comprised the satellite towns of Rheinhausen, Ruhrort, Meiderich, Hamborn and Walsum. Considered a possible target for a 'Thousand-Bomber' raid back in mid-June 1942, Bomber Command HQ had assessed that the particularly important part was the town of Duisburg itself, lying south of the River Ruhr. In stark terms, the briefing note encapsulated the thinking behind the area bombing of industrial areas and their workers:

> The administration of these industries and the life of the workers are centred on Duisburg which is a compact and congested town the liquidation of which will have a far greater effect on production than would be created by any attempt to attend to each works individually. This is to be done by overwhelming the city's military, A.R.P. and fire defences. No worker will return to work if his family is homeless. Those whose homes survive cannot get to work if the transport system is destroyed and destruction of the shopping centre not only disposes of much needed supplies but forces a general evacuation with all its consequences to surrounding industries.

This statement showed the brutal 'logic' of how a civilian population could be attacked with the city centre and its retail areas perceived as legitimate targets. The Battle of the Ruhr would see this philosophy executed to the full. The impersonal nature of killing through bombing disguised the death and agony experienced by the civilian population of many of Germany's cities, not just those in the Ruhr but also in places like Duisburg where the population particularly suffered, especially in autumn 1944. The city, like Essen, was attacked four times in the first two months by 457 aircraft on 26–27 March, 392 on 8–9 April and 109 on 9–10 April, culminating in a force of 561 bombers on 26–27 April. This huge effort saw a total of 3,606 tons of bombs dropped in an attempt to disrupt Duisburg's war production and civilian life. However, it was a frustrated endeavour: the first attack saw failures of Oboe lead to the sky-markers being scattered and, as a consequence, the bombing itself was widely dispersed throughout the sprawling city. This was ascertained from the reconnaissance photography taken by 541 Squadron on 4 and 5 April. Such images of Ruhr damage were vital for Churchill, who made a consistent effort to keep Stalin fully aware of the British bombing effort against Germany, especially during this period of considerable Anglo-Soviet tension over the launching of a Second Front in Western Europe. 'We have dropped on Duisburg 1,450 tons,' he told the Soviet premier in early May, 'the heaviest yet launched in a single raid.' This, of course, referred to the operation of 26–27 April, which saw 30 tons of bombs dropped every minute over three-quarters of an hour. Although observation by Mosquito crews bombing Duisburg several hours later reported much smoke and fire, this was not indicative of Duisburg-Ruhrort having been badly hit. Most of the bombs had fallen around the Hamborn area, which was perplexing given that the thick cloud concealing the bombers en route had cleared a few miles from the target (Bomber Command's most favoured conditions) and allowed the PFF to identify Duisburg's distinctive dock area. The weather had, moreover, hindered the night fighters, so the PFF was able to mark the aiming point particularly accurately. Yet the following Main Force crews faced Duisburg's several searchlight belts and reinforced heavy flak guns, which 'put up one of the heaviest barrages our bombers have encountered', and this may have caused crews to simply drop their bombs early, leading to considerable 'creepback' along their route into Duisburg from the north-east. Whatever the precise cause, the bombs had fallen well away from the dock area at Ruhrort.

Two back-to-back raids on Duisburg had been undertaken on 8–9 and 9–10 April, the former being the 30th operation of Charlwood's 103 Squadron crew which finally completed an operational tour. Both these attacks were ineffectual too. The first attack saw particularly bad icing in clouds up to 20,000ft and the high winds encountered en route taxed many pilots' physical strength in just maintaining a steady course. Icing probably accounted for the high rate of early returns (71 aircraft), as it made an aircraft dangerously heavy and unstable. It also caused aerials to snap off more easily, airspeed indicators to cease working properly, and the alarming sound of propellers catapulting large chunks of ice against the fuselage that unnervingly 'sounded like a succession of pistol shots'. In one case, icing proved terminal, causing the 166 Squadron Wellington of F/O Douglas Morgan to crash in the target area.

Few Main Force crews saw the PFF's sky-markers during the Musical Wanganui operation, which may have been down to a reduced number being dropped owing to some 8 Group aircraft aborting, or alternatively the very thick layer of clouds encountered between 16,000 and 23,000ft which could have simply swallowed up most of the sky-markers. Either way, most crews bombed on ETA (estimated time of arrival), a procedure that made the delivery of accurate and concentrated bombing highly unlikely. The following night, in similar weather conditions, Harris sent a force comparable to those sent against the Ruhr back in January, with five Oboe Mosquitoes leading 34 Lancasters from 1 Group and 70 from 5 Group. This small force was undertaking a 'follow-up' attack, which was the tactic of bombing the same target the night after in order to immediately add to the terror and chaos already present. However, the modest number represented all the Lancasters that could be cobbled together given the flak damage incurred by the aircraft of 1 and 5 Groups the previous night, whilst the weather was now considered too dangerous for the Halifaxes, Stirlings and Wellingtons to operate. A small-scale attack certainly kept the bombing offensive going, but sending such low numbers to a heavily defended place like the Ruhr was always likely to be risky, and 7.3 per cent were lost. Against this small raid, which was packed into 15 minutes, the German flak gunners had seemingly tried a new tactic of holding their fire until the British sky-markers went down before opening up on the portion of the sky where the flares had dropped from. This tactic, reliant on estimation, only accounted for two aircraft, however. The remainder succumbed to night fighters whilst a sixth aircraft, the 103 Squadron Lancaster of F/L Ken

Lethal flak over Duisburg: 8–9 April 1943

This scene shows the 428 'Ghost' Squadron (RCAF) Wellington X (NA-Y, HE239) of Sgt L.P. Williamson on 8–9 April, which was part of 6 Group (RCAF) and the Canadian contribution to RAF Bomber Command. Flying at 15,000ft over the huge inland port of Duisburg–Hamborn, with its characteristic landmark of the confluence of the Rhine and Ruhr rivers and its surrounding docks, the area was heavily defended by intense heavy flak and searchlight activity. Briefly caught in the lights, this depicts the moment when Williamson's Wellington, the squadron ORB noted, 'was hit by a violent burst of enemy anti-aircraft fire and the rear turret was shot completely off'. Fire broke out, burning away the Wellington's linen-based outer skin, leaving the type's distinctive metal airframe completely exposed. Despite critical damage, with half the rudder blown away, the hydraulic system rendered inoperable and bomb-bay doors unable to close, Williamson and his crew managed to get their bomber back to the UK to make an emergency landing at West Malling, minus the rear gunner, Sgt L. Bertrand, who perished in his turret. This story showed how 'bad luck' could strike individual airmen, especially in the face of the Ruhr's ferocious flak defences which, throughout the Battle of the Ruhr, particularly affected those flying in less-capable aircraft such as the two-engined Wellington. In the attack itself, the bomb damage was not concentrated in the target area of Hamborn – the site of the vast docks, quaysides and wharves of this huge inland port. Rather, fires and explosions were widely scattered throughout the vast urban conurbation of Duisburg and many other Ruhr towns. Williamson would receive the CGM for his efforts on this night.

Avro Lancaster B.Mk.III of 103 Squadron (ED724 'PM-M'), piloted by F/L K.G. Bickers, about to take off for Duisburg on 9–10 April 1943. Searchlights were being shone upwards to ascertain the height of the cloud-base. After only six operations, this particular aircraft was written off in a crash-landing at Bodney having been attacked by a night fighter. The aircraft had sustained tremendous damage – the rear-turret was set on fire, the hydraulics, WT, RT, Gee, ASI Trimmers were all beyond repair and the petrol tanks holed – but the Lancaster still got back, although the rear-gunner had been killed. (Getty Images)

Bickers, was badly shot-up over Holland, killing the rear gunner and forcing a crash-landing at Bodney aerodrome in Norfolk. Overall, the effort against Duisburg had yielded modest results for the considerable bombload dropped. Sky-marking had been used on the first three attacks, but had not provided sufficient concentration for a high level of destruction, whilst the fourth operation, made in clearer weather, was let down by bombing seemingly going astray over this sprawling town. But, like its C-in-C, Bomber Command remained undeterred and a further operation to Duisburg was undertaken on 12–13 May, with, as will be seen, quite different results.

In the opening two months, only one other Ruhr city was attacked by Bomber Command. On 27–28 April, an attack on Dortmund had been ordered, but was cancelled late in the afternoon – the city's first massive attack came a week later in early May. Instead, it was Bochum, with its vital steelworks and coal mines, that was attacked on 29–30 March, only the fourth Ruhr operation in the opening month. This hardly represented an intense beginning, and the Bochum operation was itself part of a double-attack that saw the bulk of Bomber Command's front-line strength attack Berlin, whilst a force of eight Mosquitoes and 149 Wellingtons went to the Ruhr. Sending these increasingly antiquated aircraft on their own was hardly a good decision, and 12 failed to return. But Harris was under pressure from Churchill to attack Berlin, and a specific Directive on 17 February had stated that attacks on Hitler's capital were to coincide with German setbacks on the Eastern Front (withdrawal from the Rzhev Salient), and he may have decided to keep the Wellingtons operating against Bochum to draw the German night fighters away from the force going to Berlin. Whatever the case, the Wellingtons encountered terrible weather en route, with 10–10 cloud up to 15,000ft. Despite unexpectedly cloudless conditions over the target, the PFF still commenced a Musical Wanganui attack. The resultant bombing was scattered, suggesting the sky-markers, though concentrated, were few in number and had not been well placed over Bochum, for very few buildings in the town were hit. Scattered fires and explosions were seen north of the target, but these were in the adjacent towns of Herne and Castrop Rauxel.

The Bochum raid's losses of 8 per cent were exceptionally bad, and at least partly attributable to sending an antiquated medium bomber against a heavily defended target in the Ruhr. Overall, the start of the Battle of the Ruhr Bomber Command's loss-rate increase from 2.5 per cent in February 1943 to 3.6 per cent in March, which as yet could hardly be considered heavy but nonetheless pointed to increasing losses against the Ruhr being highly likely. Breaking down the figures, the four attacks on Essen saw Bomber Command lose 14 aircraft (3.2 per cent) on 5–6 March, a noticeable rise to 23 (5.0 per cent) on 12–13 March, 21 (6.0 per cent) on 3–4 April and 12 (3.9 per cent) on 30 April–1 May. On the same number of operations against Duisburg, the figures were six aircraft lost (1.3 per cent) on 26–27 March, 19 (4.8 per cent) on 8–9 April, eight (7.3 per cent) on the following night and 17 (3.0 per cent) on 26–27 April. The loss totals were 70 and 50 aircraft; 4.5 per cent and 3.3 per cent from the 1,552 and 1,517 total aircraft despatched respectively. Generally, these losses showed the success of the Luftwaffe's night fighter pilots who patrolled the Kammhuber Line. The Battle of the Ruhr saw skilled German 'aces' add to their tallies, men like OLt Werner Streib of I/NJG-1; Hptm Wilhelm Dormann and Oblt Eckart-Wilhelm von Bonin of II/NJG-1; Hptm Herbert Lütje, Hptm Wolfgang Thimmig, Lt August Geiger,

Lt Werner Rapp and Uffz Christian Költringer of III/NJG-1; also Hptm Helmut Lent, Lt Robert Denzel, OFw Heinz Vinke and Lt Oskar Köstler of IV/NJG-1. On 26–27 April, Vinke despatched the 76 Squadron Halifax of Sgt Donald McNab (RNZAF), which crashed into the Luftwaffe's headquarters at the Carlton Hotel in Amsterdam. But these German pilots also suffered losses. On 9–10 April, Oskar Köstler shot down a 101 Squadron Lancaster piloted by WO2 John Steele (RCAF), however the bomber, probably struck in the bomb bay, exploded so violently that debris also killed the Luftwaffe pilot.

With regards to the flak, for all its noise and intensity, the picture was more mixed. It did bring down some aircraft, on average some three or four per operation, but not all from the guns located in and around the Ruhr. The coast of Holland proved especially notorious; on 8–9 April, a Wellington of 300 (Polish) Squadron was brought down by fire from a flak barge operating near the shore. Yet the guns of the Ruhr provided some crews with memorable moments, and left Bomber Command's squadrons with consistent long lists of damaged aircraft. Over Duisburg on 8–9 April, one Lancaster crew told how their aircraft 'was thrown on its back by flak which burst with a blinding flash', before falling down to 12,000ft, well below the cloud. Essen's flak caused a considerable number of aircraft to return holed and damaged: 61 on 12–13 March, 59 on 3–4 April and 45 on the fourth attack. However, the figure of just eight aircraft returning damaged from night-fighter attack on 12–13 March showed all too clearly that the Luftwaffe's pilots tended to destroy, not damage, the British bombers. Charlwood cited a vivid account given by his pilot, fellow Australian Geoff Maddern, describing the German defences and in particular the aggressiveness of the Luftwaffe's night-fighter pilots on 3–4 April. Maddern said of the crew's seventh trip to Essen and 28th operation:

> The air was alive with night fighters and bursting shells all along our route. Seventy miles from Essen we saw four machines go down in the space of two minutes. One in the target, one a few hundred yards away on our starboard; the third northwest of Essen and the last behind us as we made our way in. Others could be seen going down all around us. The searchlight cones seemed well occupied, so in we went. Hell! It was like hell in there. Fingers of light were feeling for us; shells bursting very close, bumping and rattling the fuselage. Even their night fighters were in there. About a thousand yards away I saw one kite cop a packet. He burst into flames and started going down. A fighter must have been on his tail – he kept pumping tracer into him as he was going down … . Coming home we had to corkscrew all the way. We seemed surrounded by fighters… . Everyone in the crew admitted on landing that it was the most hair-raising affair they've been on.

With such defences, it was no wonder that flying to the Ruhr, and Essen in particular, came to be dreaded.

Supporting the main battle

Behind Bomber Command's main effort there were a number of supporting operations carried out against a multitude of different targets connected to the Ruhr industrially, if not geographically. Some were conducted by the overlooked element of Bomber Command, 2 Group, which attacked specialist targets away from the Ruhr but connected with its war production. Two raids in particular stand out. The first was on 3 March, when ten Mosquitoes from 139 Squadron flew in daylight to bomb the molybdenum mines at Knaben in Norway, a target which the Air Ministry had requested in a Directive on 10 February 1943 as its raw material was critical for the process of hardening steel. Using the Mosquitoes' bombing tactic of dividing the ground defences by attacking in two formations, with one at low level and the other making a shallow dive from a higher altitude to strike the target, bombs severely damaged

Air Vice-Marshal J.H. D'Albiac, AOC 2 Group. Often overlooked, this group was still part of Bomber Command's Order of Battle until 31 May 1943 when it was transferred to the Tactical Air Force. Nonetheless, 2 Group undertook a number of daylight operations connected with the Battle of the Ruhr which included bombing the molybdenum mines at Knaben (Norway) and the massive docks of Rotterdam. (© IWM CH 10618)

The daylight raid on 3 March by 2 Group's Mosquitoes against Knaben. These mines in Norway produced molybdenum, which was vital material for the hardening of the Ruhr's steel. This product, in addition to Swedish iron ore, was shipped to Germany. Its interference would be the aim of Bomber Command's minelaying of the sea-lanes to Germany's ports, which was extensive during the Battle of the Ruhr. A record of 593 mines would be laid on 28–29 April alone. (© IWM C 5683)

the flotation plant building and the machinery inside. On 9 March, Bufton informed Bottomley that the attack was 'brilliantly executed' and 'represents the correct employment of our secondary effort against a tender spot in the German war economy'. Webster and Frankland also cite a German Economics Intelligence Branch study that stated 'much anxiety was caused to the economic staff of the Wehrmacht by this attack'.

The second notable attack by 2 Group's Mosquitoes came on 27 May. Comprising 14 aircraft from 105 and 139 Squadrons, they flew at low level in daylight right across Germany to bomb the Zeiss Factory in Jena, which made the aiming devices for Germany's flak guns and the optical instruments required for the Seeburg plotting tables.

Elsewhere, Mosquitoes from 8 Group, when not using Oboe for target-marking duties for the Main Force, conducted a range of supporting operations. These included 'spoof raids' to simulate an attack beginning elsewhere and thereby draw the night fighters to the wrong location – as seen on 13–14 July, when two Mosquitoes dropped target-markers over Cologne to mask the main attack being on Aachen – and making small-scale attacks on the Ruhr to hinder reconstruction efforts and strain civilian morale. On several occasions, Mosquitoes flew with or just behind the main bomber force to attack a specific target within the same city, such as on 26–27 April, when three hours after the main attack on Duisburg, four Mosquitoes (from 2 Group) dropped bombs no doubt to hamper the city's fire services and post-raid relief efforts. On 9–10 July, the same number of Mosquitoes, now all operating with 8 Group, attacked the Gelsenkirchen-Nordstern oil refinery whilst the main effort was directed against the city itself.

Bomber Command's four-engine bombers were no less busy in support operations. Primarily, they bombed cities away from the Ruhr to both stretch the air defences into southern and north-eastern Germany – thereby hindering the reinforcement of the Ruhr – and destroy important industrial centres elsewhere. Bomber Command thus flew long-distance operations to the politically and symbolically important targets of Nuremberg (8–9 March), Munich (9–10 March), Berlin (27–28 and 29–30 March), Frankfurt (10–11 April) and Stuttgart (11–12 March and 14–15 April). The latter contained the Bosch electrical equipment plant and the Daimler-Benz engine works, so bombing Stuttgart simultaneously with the Ruhr made sense in the overall aim of breaking the German war economy. The MEW also believed the damage to Krupps now meant the huge Skoda armament works in Pilsen had become increasingly important to the German war economy, and major attacks were attempted there on 16–17 April and 13–14 May by 327 and 156 aircraft respectively.

Representing round-trips of 1,900 miles by Lancasters carrying maximum fuel loads (2,154 gallons), the plan called for bombing the factory from between 4,000 and 6,000ft, but both attacks were considerable failures because H2S could not provide a definite outline of the target. Losses in the first raid were especially severe at 11 per cent (36 aircraft), with 51 Squadron alone losing five Halifaxes, owing to the full moon aiding the German night fighters and ground defences. The second operation saw further problems of locating the factory, and bombs fell in open countryside several miles north of Pilsen, albeit in an impressively concentrated pattern. Other important industrial targets in Axis-controlled Europe bombed during this campaign were the Schneider Works in Le Creusot (19–20 June), the Fiat factories in Turin (12–13 July) and the Peugeot plant at Montbéliard (15–16 July).

The second aspect of the supporting missions was the bombing of Germany's Baltic ports, such as Stettin and Kiel (by 338 and 577 aircraft on 20–21 April and 4–5 April respectively), which were vital for supplying Germany's armies in the East and for unloading critical raw materials shipped from Scandinavia.

The need to stop German and Swedish shipping also saw a considerable minelaying effort undertaken, especially during late April, to interrupt the Swedish iron ore supplies consumed by the Ruhr's heavy industries. In one 48-hour period, over 1,000 mines were dropped by a total of 367 bombers in German shipping lanes, especially around the Dutch Islands, Heligoland Bight and the Elbe Estuary, the Danish Belts, Kiel Bay and north German coast. This effort at sea was no coincidence, given that Harris had just attacked Germany's largest inland port, Duisburg. It came at a cost, however. The minelaying operation on 28–29 April suffered losses of 10.6 per cent (22 aircraft), mostly due to light flak along coastal areas, and 12 Squadron and 75 Squadron lost four Lancasters and four Stirlings respectively. Bombing and minelaying operations around the Baltic were stopped from late April, however, because these were expected to be even more costly as 'the northern sky was sufficiently light to silhouette aircraft even on a dark night'. Indeed, from this time, options for diversionary attacks away from the Ruhr became much more limited, as the summer nights not only ruled out the Baltic ports but Berlin, targets in southern Germany, Frankfurt and northern Italy; instead, the only possibility was industrial targets in France. Nonetheless, as will be seen, the implications for the Luftwaffe's defence of the Ruhr would prove considerable.

Harris also undertook further 'test' raids of H2S, with operations to Münster (11–12 June) and Cologne (16–17 June). The Münster attack was made by just 72 H2S-equipped aircraft from 8 Group to give further operational experience of using this device and trial a new method of coloured marking. Hitherto, visual ground-marking saw the same colour TIs being dropped by the visual-markers and 'backers-up', but this could confuse the Main Force who had little idea of which corresponded to the proper marker on which to drop their bombs. Thus, ground-marking was now to comprise three colours: yellow for blind-markers, red for visual-markers and green for the 'backers-up'. This new approach to marking, coupled with H2S, meant 57 per cent of the attacking force dropped their bombs within three miles of the aiming-point. Yet Münster was an exceptionally favourable target for H2S, being small and surrounded by countryside, which meant it showed up reasonably clearly on the operator's screen. Much less clear were the larger cities (Berlin) that filled the entire screen or sprawling, indistinct urban areas (the Ruhr). H2S led the attack on Cologne on 16–17 June, with 8 Group's Halifaxes using it for a sky-marking attack in thick cloud up to 20,000ft, but it was not a success and served to highlight just how vital Oboe was.

Stettin was bombed on 20–21 April 1943. This target was attacked because it was a tactical diversion away from the Ruhr area and also a major supply port for German forces in Russia. Some 600 miles from the UK, Stettin was well beyond Oboe range and H2S had to be used. Though a difficult instrument to use, whose mercurial traits had led to a scattered attack on Pilsen four nights earlier, the Stettin operation was Bomber Command's most successful long-range attack during the Battle of the Ruhr. This was because H2S could make accurate distinctions between the sea and land. (© IWM C 3513)

'Maximum effort' at Dortmund and the 'real catastrophe' of Wuppertal, May 1943

On 2 May 1943, Harris went to Chequers for the regular Sunday night dinner with Churchill, and on this occasion, the prime minister asked for a list of all the major Germans towns and their population size. Supposedly, this was to have been provided by the Air Ministry, but

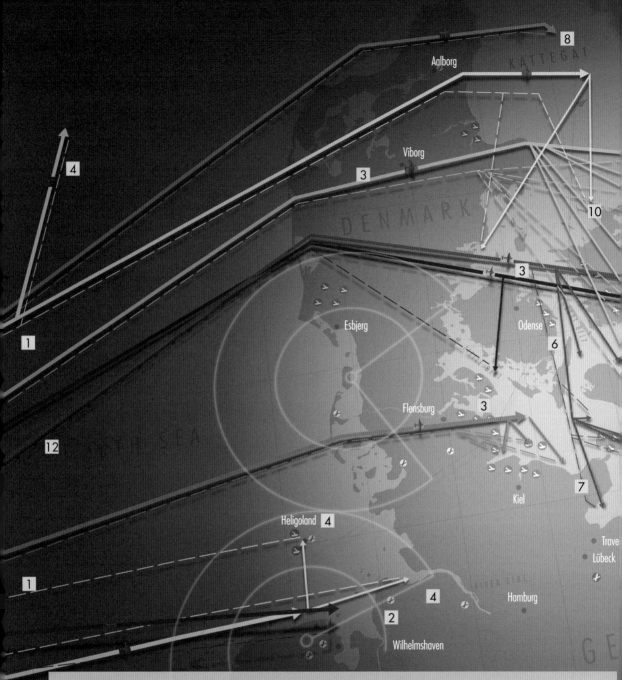

Aalborg

KATTEGAT

8

Viborg

3

DENMARK

10

4

Esbjerg

Odense

1

6

12

Flensburg

3

3

7

Kiel

NORTH SEA

Trave

Lübeck

Heligoland

4

1

RIVER ELBE

Hamburg

4

2

Wilhelmshaven

GE

EVENTS

1. 2200–2245hrs: formations of British aircraft cross the North Sea and approach the north-west coast of Germany and the west coast of Denmark. 232 aircraft – the largest minelaying operation of the war – from all Bomber Groups are dispatched.

2. 2243–2300hrs: six Mosquitoes from 2 Group undertake a diversionary attack on Wilhelmshaven. Not equipped with Oboe, three aircraft release flares and the others drop 500lb MC bombs.

3. 2230–2330hrs: low cloud at 2,000–3,000ft is encountered by the bomber forces over most of the routes and areas concerned, which causes the attacking aircraft to lose height. Visibility below the cloud is

good, thus enabling the attacking forces to commence their minelaying operations.

4. 2259–2337hrs: 18 Wellington Xs from 6 (RCAF) Group undertake the mining of waters near Haugesund in Norway (not shown on BEV), in the estuary of the River Elbe, and around Heligoland. Light flak claims two aircraft on the latter target.

5. 2329–0057hrs: 3 Group's 22 Stirlings and two Lancaster Mk.IIs drop their mines in the Great Belt, Langeland Belt, Cadet Channel, and Fehmarn Channel. Eight Stirlings lost to light flak and German fighters throughout this wide area.

Stopping Germany's raw materials from Sweden: the minelaying operation, 28–29 April 1943

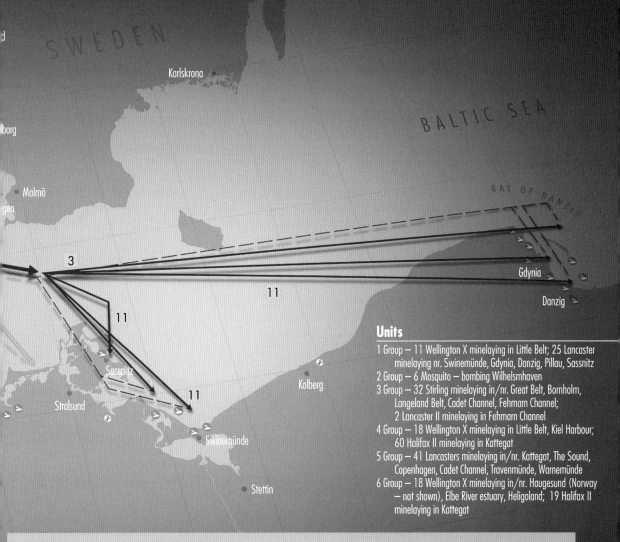

Units

1 Group – 11 Wellington X minelaying in Little Belt; 25 Lancaster minelaying nr. Swinemünde, Gdynia, Danzig, Pillau, Sassnitz

2 Group – 6 Mosquito – bombing Wilhelsmhaven

3 Group – 32 Stirling minelaying in/nr. Great Belt, Bornholm, Langeland Belt, Cadet Channel, Fehmarn Channel; 2 Lancaster II minelaying in Fehmarn Channel

4 Group – 18 Wellington X minelaying in Little Belt, Kiel Harbour; 60 Halifax II minelaying in Kattegat

5 Group – 41 Lancasters minelaying in/nr. Kattegat, The Sound, Copenhagen, Cadet Channel, Travenmünde, Warnemünde

6 Group – 18 Wellington X minelaying in/nr. Haugesund (Norway – not shown), Elbe River estuary, Heligoland; 19 Halifax II minelaying in Kattegat

EVENTS

6. 2337–2350hrs: 1 Group's nine Wellington Xs commence minelaying operations in the Little Belt. One lost to light flak.

7. 2345–0004hrs: twelve Wellington Xs of 4 Group drop their mines in the Little Belt and in Kiel Harbour. Alert enemy; light-flak defences around Kiel Bay claim three aircraft.

8. 2347–0101hrs: 56 Halifax IIs (4 Group) lay mines throughout the Kattegat, including off the northern tip of Denmark (not shown on BEV). One shot down by a German fighter.

9. 2350–0143hrs: 5 Group's 37 Lancasters drop their mines throughout the Kattegat, The Sound, the Cadet Channel, and in waters near Copenhagen, Travenmünde, and Warnemünde. One Lancaster is shot down by a German fighter near Copenhagen, and another is claimed over The Sound.

10. 2352–0040hrs: 14 Halifaxes from 6 Group drop mines throughout their assigned areas in the Kattegat.

11. 0023–0220hrs: meanwhile travelling much further east are 1 Group's 17 Lancasters to conduct their minelaying of the waters near Swinemünde, Sassnitz, Gdynia, Danzig, and Pillau (nr. Königsburg). Light flak brings down two Lancasters near Swinemünde and three around the Bay of Danzig.

12. All bomber forces return to the UK over the North Sea. 182 aircraft have completed the operation, laying a total of 593 mines in the sea-lanes from Scandinavia to Germany. But it proves an expensive night with 23 aircraft lost (10.2%), the majority coming from coastal light flak guns or those mounted on ships. HQ Bomber Command conducts an investigation into the losses and concludes the routes passed too close to heavily-defended coastal zones, with low-flying over these areas, and the strengthening of these flak defences, especially in the south-western Baltic, 'as part of increased protection for Berlin', which had been attacked three times in March 1943 contributing. Although Bomber Command's most expensive minelaying operation of the war, the number of mines dropped would be a record.

Specialist attacks

Although the twin-engined Mosquito was regularly undertaking the precision bombing of specific targets, this approach, when adopted by the four-engined Lancaster, led to the most famous attack of the Battle of the Ruhr, indeed Bomber Command's entire war. Much has been written on Operation *Chastise*: the development of a radical new weapon ('Upkeep'), the formation of a specially trained squadron for the task under the legendary Wg Cdr Guy Gibson, the modifications needed by the Lancasters, and ultimately the bravery and sacrifice of 617 Squadron aircrews on the operation itself. Famously, it also meant overcoming Harris' objections; in mid-February 1943, he had described Barnes Wallis' 'bouncing bomb' as 'tripe of the wildest description' that held 'not the smallest chance of success' (although the C-in-C became more disposed to the operation once the bomb had been successfully tested). With this in mind, the operation to destroy the Ruhr dams cannot be seen as anything less than a spectacular achievement, but, for all its fame, this was an operation designed to achieve the overriding aim of knocking out the Ruhr industries, albeit by using a radically different approach.

Even before September 1939, the observation had been made in the Air Ministry that the Ruhr's industries were reliant on the reservoirs held behind the Möhne, Eder and Sorpe dams, whose destruction, so they thought, would seriously interfere with war production, flood the local countryside, wash away vital railway lines and restrict domestic water consumption. On 28 March 1943, the Air Staff stated that breaching the Möhne dam would seriously hamper 'the foundries, coal mines, coke ovens, blast furnaces and chemical plants which require enormous quantities of water for their operation', whilst collapsing the Sorpe dam would simply have a 'paralysing' effect on the Ruhr's industries. *Chastise* went ahead on 16–17 May, and destroyed the Möhne and Eder dams, but the Sorpe and Schwelme dams remained. It proved to be a 'one-shot' operation. Using 'Upkeep' had exposed 617 Squadron to huge risks: 42.1 per cent were lost owing to light flak and low-flying clashes, both en route and from dropping the bouncing bomb at its critical release altitude of just 60ft. Such losses prevented, and probably dissuaded, a further attack on the Sorpe dam, particularly as its light-flak defences were bound to have been reinforced. Yet for the loss of eight aircraft, Bomber Command had succeeded in creating quite a mess. The collapsed Möhne dam released 137 million gallons of water from the River Ruhr which drowned 1,294 people (including 493 foreign workers) and caused a lowering, if only temporary, of water consumption in the Ruhr. Breaching the Eder dam saw 210 million gallons of water cause considerable flooding of surrounding agricultural land and even of Kassel's suburbs. Repair consumed colossal amounts of concrete and labour (some 20,000 workers from the Todt Organization), which was diverted from other massive projects, such as the Atlantic Wall fortifications. For Bomber Command itself, the Dams Raid saw 617 Squadron's experience of specialist training and operations spread throughout its parent unit, 5 Group, which developed new tactics and techniques to allow its operation as an independent component within the bomber force from spring 1944.

Before the Battle of the Ruhr ended, 5 Group made another special attack called Operation *Bellicose*. The impetus behind it was the Germans' Giant Würzburg radar, and the recommendations of the British scientist, Professor R. V. Jones, who saw photographic evidence that these were made at the old Zeppelin Works in Friedrichshafen. Jones asked Churchill's scientific adviser, Lord Cherwell, to persuade Churchill to order an attack. But Friedrichshafen lay in southern Germany, on Lake Constance, and the summer nights meant the attacking force – 60 Lancasters from 5 Group – had to fly on to North African bases. Such an operation was called a 'shuttle attack', and allowed the bombing of a target in Italy on the bombers' return journey. Requiring considerable precision to bomb specific factory sites, *Bellicose* involved some new techniques: a 'Master Bomber' to direct the first wave, whilst the second wave pioneered 5 Group's technique of making 'time-and-distance' runs from a notable landmark, in this case Lake Constance. Accuracy was achieved, with heavy destruction to the Zeppelin Works and adjoining Maybach tank-engine factory. Jones, whose work at this time was consumed by defeating the Kammhuber Line, was pleased at the bombing blow struck on the Würzburgs' manufacture. Intelligence also informed Jones that damage was done to part of the Zeppelin Works earmarked for V-2 production.

by 8 May, hearing it had not been sent, Harris did so. This came at a critical moment, for it was two months into the Ruhr air campaign and allowed Harris to tell Churchill directly about Bomber Command's achievements, at a time when others, particularly the Royal Navy, were pressing for a greater concentration on targets connected with the war at sea. In a cover note, the C-in-C gleefully wrote that the plot of night photographs from the recent raid against Dortmund (4–5 May) showed 'one of the most promising concentrations we have ever achieved and I am confident that when we get the day photographic cover it will reveal great damage'. This was all designed to re-emphasize his view that area bombing remained the most effective bombing strategy, for Harris was aware that some in the Air Ministry were advocating a shift towards attacks on particular industrial sites; indeed, a Directive requesting attacks on Schweinfurt's ball-bearing factories would be issued on 26 May. Later confirmation indicated that the attack on Dortmund, the Ruhr's most easterly town, had been successful, with a 4,000lb bomb having fallen every 23 seconds. These, together with some 8,000-pounders, had caused severe damage to the city centre and northern districts, although not all the bombing fell around the aiming-point. Harris needed the good results from the Dortmund raid as this period of prime ministerial interest in the air campaign awkwardly coincided with few attacks on the Ruhr; from 1–2 to 11–12 May, an operation against Duisburg was cancelled six times.

Duisburg was eventually attacked on 12–13 May, when 572 aircraft destroyed the city centre and port area, which were consumed by immense fires that continued to burn the following day. The excellent visibility had allowed the PFF aircraft to see Duisburg, which was probably the most visually distinctive target in the Ruhr. Handily for Harris, the bomb tonnage dropped was a record, with the 1,559 tons (905 HEs and 654 IBs) surpassing the 1,516 tons dropped in the 'Thousand-Bomber' attack on Cologne in mid-1942, and was a great advert for the expanding capabilities of Bomber Command. Fewer but better aircraft had delivered more bombs to Germany, more accurately and in much less time. Continuing the momentum, the following night, British bombers attacked the last major Ruhr city that had remained relatively untouched, Bochum, which was soon engulfed in fires that were seen by those crews returning from the second Pilsen operation. Photo Reconnaissance Unit (PRU) sorties, undertaken by 542 Squadron on 15 May, delivered photographs that were examined at the Central Interpretation Unit (CIU) at RAF Medmenham, before various Interpretation Reports were released. From this information, the MEW and the Ministry of Home Security's RE8 Department would conduct detailed examination of an attack's effects. In this instance, the latter concluded that 69 per cent of the visible damage had occurred in three out of the four Bochumer Verein steelworks. The area of damage in the three plants totalled 432,000 sqft, causing an estimated loss of 7,000 tons of crude steel and 31,000 tons of high-grade steel, which equated to some 1.4 per cent of the estimated yearly production. These methods, however – based on calculations, estimates and guesswork – left considerable scope for errors.

Nevertheless, this sort of analysis led to assessments by the MEW on what targets Bomber Command should be attacking. On 13 May, the RE8 Department produced a paper arguing that 'the most immediate' priority was Germany's arms production. Requiring Krupps and Rheinmetall-Borsig to be 'permanently immobilized', it also needed the manufacture of aircraft, aero-engines, tanks and vehicles elsewhere in Germany to be severely disrupted by mounting heavy attacks on the Ruhr towns engaged in producing 'special steels' which 'could not adequately' be produced elsewhere. The MEW thus suggested to the Air Ministry's Directorate of Bomber Operations a more focused bombing programme that comprised:

The biggest operation: Dortmund 23–24 May 1943

On 23–24 May, Bomber Command launched its largest operation in the Battle of the Ruhr, when its entire front-line strength of 826 aircraft was sent to attack Dortmund. Depicted are two Lancaster IIIs from 103 Squadron, dropping their bombs on the north-eastern part of this major Ruhr city. The lower-flying aircraft PM-L (ED884) was piloted by Sgt S.F. Gage, and the Lancaster at the higher altitude of 21,000ft PM-X (ED905) was skippered by F/O Florent van Rollegham, DSO DFC, with its distinctive nose art of crossed Belgian and British flags. In clear weather over Dortmund, both aircraft dropped their bombs towards the end of the attack, when the target area around the massive Hoesch Steelworks was blazing furiously. Van Rollegham's aircraft has just released a standard bombload for an area attack, namely a 1× 4,000lb 'cookie', with its distinctive large drum-like shape, 6× 500lb GP bombs, 2× 250lb, and several packs of incendiaries. Originally from Belgium, and a former member of the local resistance who escaped to Britain, van Rollegham was a brave, determined pilot, with shades of being something of a maverick. Going on to complete a staggering 70 operations in three tours for 103 Squadron in just 18 months, van Rollegham was awarded both a DSO and a DFC, and had to be ordered off operations by the Belgian government-in-exile in late October 1944. He was considered too valuable to lose, for he had been earmarked for a major role in the rebuilding of the post-war Belgian Air Force. This he did, rising to high rank. He also became a very senior figure in NATO. He was one of many Europeans who joined Bomber Command owing to their countries having come under German occupation. He died in 1983. (The author would like to acknowledge Mr David Fell, 103 Squadron Association, for his information on van Rollegham.)

Major Cities:

1. Essen (special steels and heavy engineering)
2. Düsseldorf (special steels and heavy engineering)
3. Bochum (open-hearth and special steels)
4. Duisburg (open-hearth steels)
5. Dortmund (open-hearth steels)

Minor Cities:

1. Krefeld (special steels)
2. Remscheid (special steels)
3. Witten (open-hearth and special steels)
4. Hattingen (open-hearth steels)

This programme also required 'frequent raids' on the Ruhr's coke ovens and blast furnaces, while the 'incidental damage' on housing and transport from these area attacks was believed to cause an estimated 20–25 per cent reduction in coal output owing to 'absenteeism and transport dislocation'. A further reduction in coal and steel production of 5–10 per cent could materialize from frequent air-raid alerts by 'interspersing feint attacks between the mass attacks'. Initially, it is difficult to see this as being much different from what Harris was already doing to the Ruhr, yet does this explain Bomber Command's target selection over the final months of the Ruhr campaign? Certainly, attacks on the smaller 'special steel'-producing Ruhr towns would be undertaken in June and July, whilst the Mosquitoes' small-scale attacks would be intensified.

Perhaps this was symbolic of some believing the Battle of the Ruhr lacked a more definite purpose, and needed more specific direction. With the campaign itself having become sluggish over the previous two weeks, comprising just three major attacks, the simultaneous rise of doubts and specific targets could not have come at a worse moment for Harris. Needing Portal's support, Harris wrote in typically exaggerated fashion on 15 May that 'staggering destruction had been inflicted throughout the Ruhr to an extent that no nation could stick for long', which, if maintained, 'cannot fail to be lethal'. Portal received this letter at an Anglo–American conference in Washington, and knowing the Americans were pressing for a different approach to target selection, which soon emerged as the Pointblank Directive, Harris was keen to supply arguments for the continuation of area bombing. Harris needed – and quickly – a spectacular example of area bombing on an industrial city. This meant a 'maximum effort', and for several days the bomber force was conserved for this. The ORB (Operational Record Book) of 83 Squadron noted that 18–19 May was 'perfect weather conditions', but there were 'no operations', and this was the same the following day. Successive days of no operations meant that, by 23–24 May, Harris could send 826 aircraft in the campaign's largest attack, a record not surpassed until the Berlin operation of 15–16 February 1944 (891 aircraft). Setting off to bomb Dortmund, the force saw a record number dispatched by 8 Group, with 83, 97 and 156 Squadrons, plus the PFF's Lancaster units, operating together for the first time. Incredibly, the first wave itself comprised 250 bombers, with over 550 set to follow in successive formations. The figures for such a force are simply staggering: some 1.8 million gallons of petrol, 60,000 gallons of oil, 4,000 gallons of engine coolant, 9 million rounds of .303in ammunition and over 2,000 tons of HE and incendiary bombs. These bombs brought huge destruction to northern and eastern Dortmund, the city's areas of steel production, which were engulfed by vast fires, huge smoke columns and numerous large explosions,

A jovial Halifax crew from 51 Squadron return their parachutes after a successful trip to the Ruhr. (© IWM CH 10293)

with one bomb erupting up to 15,000ft. Upon hearing the news, Goebbels wrote the attack had been:

extraordinarily heavy, probably the worst ever directed against a German city … Reports from Dortmund are horrible. The critical things about it is that industrial and munitions plants have been hit very hard. One can only repeat about air warfare: we are in a position of almost helpless inferiority and must grin and bear it as we take the blows.

Two nights later, 759 bombers were sent to Düsseldorf, the Rhineland city that represented a new target for Bomber Command during the Battle of the Ruhr. Subjected to three heavy attacks in 1942, the MEW, RE8 and Bomber Command HQ all believed that by spring 1943 the reconstruction efforts meant Düsseldorf had recovered and now fully functioned as a major centre of war production. But the attack proved disappointing. Inexplicably, the Oboe sky-marking failed completely, and although some bombed on the markers, many did so on the estimated centre of the TIs, and others did a timed-run from the PFF's route-markers. The bombing was scattered over a wide area, and Düsseldorf – in Webster and Frankland's somewhat brutal description – 'survived only to have its heart torn out on the night of 11th June'.

On 27–28 May, a force was dispatched to bomb Essen again – the last time having been over three weeks before – with the 518 bombers organized into ten waves, each one carrying a bombload calculated to do 'the most damage at each stage of the attack', which lasted from 0045hrs to 0135hrs. Because of its sheer vastness over 800 acres, the Krupp Works was, it was felt, still in need of further attack. The Musical Wanganui method was adopted, and the PFF's crews maintained a continuous supply of sky-markers thanks to the ten Mosquitoes being supplemented by two reserve aircraft, designated for marking duties if the Oboe equipment failed in any of the others. In the event, one reserve Mosquito was required, but the marking became more erratic with ten- and seven-minute intervals followed by one-minute gaps, when the plan had stipulated an equal spacing of five minutes for each Mosquito. Owing to this, incendiaries were scattered north of the aiming-point and it was discovered later that only relatively light damage had occurred in Essen's northern suburbs, whilst bombs had fallen in many neighbouring towns. The bomber crews observed many explosions, with one so huge that it was seen 100 miles away by those on their homeward journey, but this was not indicative of the Krupp Works being vaporized.

Instead, the real success of late May was the attack on Barmen, the eastern half of Wuppertal, which marked the beginning of the Ruhr's smaller towns being attacked. Whilst the adjoining

A bitter incident: Düsseldorf, 25–26 May 1943

Harris' operational policy of tightly concentrating the bomber-stream may have had the advantages of overwhelming a target's flak and searchlight defences and, later, protecting as many aircraft as possible behind their Window screen, but so many bombers flying in the dark so close carried dangers too. One was the very obvious risk of collision, with aircrews frequently reporting their own aircraft violently shaking from passing another's slipstream, and certainly in the very hectic target area the threat from collision became even higher, as did the risk from being struck by bombs dropped by a higher-flying bomber. The other danger was the one depicted in this scene. After several British aircraft had completed their bombing of Düsseldorf on 25–26 May and were leaving the target area, heading for Jülich near the Dutch–German border, the 77 Squadron Halifax II (KN-D, JB837) piloted by Sgt R. Lewis was attacked by a night fighter at 17,000ft, and blew up in an almighty explosion. With debris going in all directions, the huge blast brought down two Stirling IIIs flying nearby, one from 7 Squadron (MG-B, EF361) piloted by P/O J.E.G.F. Berthiaume (RCAF) and the other skippered by F/O I.S. Thomson (RCAF) of 15 Squadron (LS-L, BF534), which had its tail sliced clean off. There were no survivors, and six out of the 18 who perished were from the Royal Canadian Air Force. These were three of the 27 aircraft lost on this operation, which ultimately was unsuccessful because the Pathfinders found layer-cloud had obstructed the aiming-point. With the marking being inaccurate, only a few scattered fires occurred in Düsseldorf and the nearby town of Neuss.

Elberfeld could be considered the industrial part, Barmen was an old town comprising narrow and congested streets and a high percentage of timbered buildings. Against this small target, 719 aircraft carrying maximum bombloads totalling 1,500 tons were sent; the result of such a force's bombs mostly dropping within a 1-mile radius of the aiming-point could only ever be catastrophic. In fact, the attack nearly went awry. The opening red TIs were late but accurately placed, however for 18 minutes no others fell. The attack was saved by the 'backers-up' of 83 and 156 Squadrons and their accurately dropped greens TIs, along with the inflammable nature of this old town's centre. A considerable proportion of the aircraft flying alongside the 'backers-up' carried mostly incendiaries. No doubt Wuppertal's light air defences – in theory the city was defended by the searchlights and flak guns of Cologne and Düsseldorf – had allowed bomb-aimers to focus on accurately releasing their markers and bombs without being distracted by the dazzling bright white searchlight beams or the alarming cracks of flak shells exploding nearby. Consequently, the 'greens' and IBs that were dropped helped concentrate the bombing of subsequent waves onto the right area, and soon numerous fires began merging into one giant conflagration, with a 'firestorm' engulfing the *Altstadt*. Aircrews in the last wave found Wuppertal had completely disappeared in the thick smoke that rose to 15,000ft. The people and city of Wuppertal-Barmen really suffered from this attack: some 3,400 were killed, 119,000 became homeless, an estimated 34,000 dwellings were destroyed and over 1,000 acres (or 83 per cent) of the built-up area perished. The main railway station, two power stations, two gasworks and the town's waterworks were knocked out. Although overshadowed by the fiery destruction of Hamburg two months later, the operation to Wuppertal-Barmen proved as Professor Richard Overy states 'one of the most effective area attacks ever launched by Bomber Command', but reflected the grim side of the British strategic bombing campaign against Germany, which in today's context is certainly abhorrent.

A target was clearly chosen not for its critical importance to the German war economy, but simply to terrorize and kill German civilians. One RAF intelligence officer, who conducted the operation briefing at 166 Squadron, later wrote: 'As I remember it, the towns [Barmen and Elberfeld] were filled with refugees from the dam busting raid, so it was not surprising that subsequent reports of casualties indicated a heavy loss of life.' Judged by its post-raid Bulletin, the Air Ministry certainly believed Wuppertal's population 'may have greatly increased in the last few months, since it is one of the few big areas in the Ruhr district which had not been attacked before'.

The bombing of Wuppertal-Barmen highlights that ruthlessness, itself a nebulous concept, was not just a German, Japanese or Soviet characteristic in World War II. Many examples can be found on the British (and American) side, including a considerable number of examples from Bomber Command's campaign: Lübeck, Wuppertal, Hamburg and Darmstadt being some of the most notorious. Wuppertal's 'other' half did not escape: 94 per cent of Elberfeld's urban area was destroyed by 630 bombers on 24–25 June, with some 1,800 being killed. Wuppertal's total death rate was approximately 5,200, which was 23.4 per cent of the 22,200 German civilians killed in the Battle of the Ruhr between March and June.

The Wuppertal inferno came at a time when Goebbels was writing about the domestic political crisis in Germany. The worsening public mood owing to Germany's war situation and the inaction of Reichsmarschall Hermann Göring and his Luftwaffe was discussed on 25 May under

Famous for its unique overhead railway – an impressive engineering feat – Wuppertal's twin-towns of Barmen and Elberfeld were attacked in two separate raids on 29–30 May and 24–25 June 1943 respectively. The first, in particular, was devastating because of the 'firestorm' (infamously more associated with Hamburg) that engulfed its old city centre. (Getty Images)

the heading of the 'Göring crisis'. Whilst Wuppertal smouldered, Goebbels noted on 30 May that Göring was 'staying in his father's castle and simply letting things go whichever way they want'. Goebbels, in contrast, as chairman of the Air Raid Damage Committee, was galvanizing the civilian effort against British raids on the Ruhr, whilst as Propaganda Minister he continued to shore up national morale in the face of the increasingly deadly aerial threat.

Meanwhile, Bomber Command began to see steeper losses. The Ruhr's ground defences had become formidable. One Stirling pilot, attacking Dortmund on 4–5 May, described how a huge belt of 200 searchlights formed giant cones. The experience of a violent flak barrage was apparent in the post-operation interrogation of a Halifax flight engineer who reported:

> Shells were bursting all round and leaving black puffs of smoke. The Halifax shook with concussion. I walked down the fuselage to the flare chute. Usually the aircraft is steadier than a bus, but this time I was thrown from side to side as the shells exploded near us, and I heard the rattle of bits of metal hitting the bomber.

Being struck by flak or subject to near misses must have been a terrifying experience. Flying over Dortmund at 19,000ft, the 156 Squadron Lancaster of Flt Lt Alastair Lang DFC took a direct hit that sent it downwards out of control; as the dive steepened, the fuselage broke apart and catapulted the two survivors, Lang and flight engineer Sgt Jack Clark DFM, out of the doomed aircraft, the other crew perishing, probably unable to get out due to G-forces. Some aircraft would suffer flak damage, before being finished off by a night fighter over or just outside the target area.

Despite their efforts, however, German guns shot down relatively few British aircraft. Sometimes hampered by thick cloud, the flak and searchlights were frequently described as intense at the beginning of a raid but slackening and becoming less accurate as the attack progressed, a clear indication that Bomber Command's tactics of saturating the defences worked.

Instead, it was the Luftwaffe's night fighter pilots who added considerably to their personal 'kill' tallies during May 1943. It should be remembered that part of Bomber Command's defensive capabilities was an ability to use the cover of darkness to evade the German night fighters. Yet this was happening less; the British formations were being detected owing to the radar capabilities of the Kammhuber Line and then intercepted more frequently. Lighter nights meant Bomber Command's tactic of raiding other parts of Germany to spread the Luftwaffe and flak defences was no longer possible, with the last one being on 20–21 April (Stettin).

The account of Hptm Wilhelm Johnen shows how the Luftwaffe was only too aware of this limitation of Bomber Command, and deployed its night fighters accordingly. Posted the previous winter with III/NJG-1 to Parchim airbase in Mecklenburg, by May 1943 this deployment was unnecessary as Berlin could no longer be reached by British bombers in darkness. Soon, 1 Jagddivision requested reinforcements for the west. 'Since in the short summer nights only attacks on the Ruhr could be envisaged', Johnen wrote, 'Fighter Corps assembled the experienced crews on the Dutch and Belgian airfields. I, too, was posted to the west.' The Luftwaffe's High Command was shuffling its forces, with its seasoned units manning the Kammhuber Line and replaced further east by the less-experienced or newly forming units.

Thus, Johnen's three-man crew, with a wireless-set, washing kit and the all-important toilet utensils, 'Schnapps cupboard' plus dog all crammed into their Bf 110, moved to Holland to join their NJG-1 comrades, spread over four wings: I/NJG-1 based at Venlo; II/NJG-1 at Sint-Truiden; III/NJG-1 at Twenthe; and IV/NJG-1 at Twenthe. Aerial 'kills' soon followed. NJG-1's pilots downed some 17 aircraft (from a total of 38 missing) over Holland on 23–24 May, with seasoned aces Lent, Thimmig, Augenstein, Vinke, Grimm,

Luftwaffe aircrew playing chess as they wait for battle with the British bombers. Despite Bomber Command's high losses, accounts by Luftwaffe veterans do recall the alertness, skill and aggression of British air-gunners. Air combat did not always yield the one-sided result of the British aircraft being shot down, as perhaps is often commonly supposed. In countering both the Americans by day and the British by night, the strain and fatigue on German aircrews was colossal. (Getty Images)

Rapp, Leuchs and Vollköpf all adding to their totals. On 25–26 May, at least four British aircraft were lost to night fighters off the French, Belgian and Dutch coasts – suggesting some interceptions were much earlier, over the North Sea – with victories for Telge, Ehle, Meurer and Greiner. The Wuppertal operation saw losses of 33 bombers – 103 Squadron flight engineer Flt Sgt Norman Ashton described how 'the "Reaper" was busy on all sides but we managed to evade his chopper' – with at least 22 being lost to night fighters. In quick succession, Schnaufer shot down four aircraft, and Meurer three. One of these was the Halifax of Sgt Charles Surgey (158 Squadron), who came from Montevideo in Uruguay – a testimony to the global recruitment of Bomber Command. May's operations (not including the Essen operation on 30 April–1 May) had cost the RAF 219 aircraft, with some units having endured a torrid time: 35 Squadron lost nine aircraft, with four on 29–30 May alone. Meanwhile, 51 Squadron endured even worse with 14 missing, including four each on 12–13 May and 23–24 May, 75 Squadron lost four Stirlings on 29–30 May and the Wellington squadrons of 6 (RCAF) Group suffered eight aircraft missing on 12–13 May. But in a testimony to the strength of British aircraft production and aircrew replenishment programmes, 51 Squadron, like other units, continued to receive reinforcements of aircraft and trained personnel, and as a result never collapsed. In this battle of attrition against industrial Germany, Bomber Command kept going through the mobilization of vast materiel and manpower resources from across the globe. This was a good job, for Harris' casualty rates were about to get worse.

The bitter battles of June

June, the fourth month of the campaign, saw an immediate downturn in British fortunes. One half of the month brought cancellations and stand-downs brought about by unfavourable weather at the bases or along the route. When, on 6–7 June, a joint operation against Münster and Oberhausen was scrubbed right before the main briefing began, this eighth consecutive non-operational day led to 'howls of dismay' amongst 83 Squadron aircrews. Frustration continued over the next three nights – the intended targets being Münster, Mülheim and Essen – after which a stand-down was ordered to give the armourers a complete rest. The consecutive cancelled operations may have frustrated the aircrews, but for those responsible for placing the bombloads in and out of the aircraft, this was simply fruitless work. In late July, 1 Group ordered a change in 'de-bombing procedure', with stations now being able to keep their Lancasters 'bombed-up' for 48 hours, although the aircraft allotted for crew training and night-flying tests still had their bombs removed and manhandled onto trolleys for storage in specially designated areas. The armourers and groundcrews always were the overlooked members of Bomber Command.

Meanwhile, on 3 June, Harris asked his Group Commanders to keep sending skilled and experienced volunteers to replenish 617 Squadron, which he wanted to maintain 'for the performance of similar tasks in the future'. 'Failure' to keep the unit going, he continued, 'would involve a serious loss to our capacity to strike telling blows at the enemy'. Some days later, the Air Staff discussed the follow-up operations to *Chastise*. They focused on a MEW report that had referenced 'the necessity of reinforcing the effects of our present policy of an "all-out" offensive against the Ruhr' by attacking the shiplifts, canal embankments and locks of the Dortmund–Ems and Mittelland canals. On these were transported vital materials and products to and from the Ruhr. Were they to be disrupted, the Air Staff believed, Germany would have to rely on its railways, 'thereby adding to the congestion of the main routes running Eastwards out of the Ruhr', particularly the Ruhr–Hamm–Bielefeld–Hannover and Ruhr–Soest–Paderborn–Altenbeken routes. Whilst Harris often exaggerated the effects of bombing, the Air Staff was not immune from doing this either, arguing that:

> The cutting of these water and rail routes simultaneously would result in the complete disruption of communications connecting the major industrial areas of Germany, and must have a disastrous effect on the whole German war effort; particularly as the weight of rail and water traffic reaches its highest peak in Germany between the months of August and October.

Thus, 617 Squadron's new targets were the Rothensee Shiplift on the Mittelland Canal, raised embankments at certain strategic points on both canals, and the Bielefeld and Paderborn Viaducts, which it was proposed to attack simultaneously with 25 'Upkeep' aircraft and the 'special' Mosquitoes of 618 Squadron, and certainly 617 Squadron would attack these targets in the autumn. Nonetheless, the Air Ministry's overall aim was 'increasing disorganization in the Ruhr', and Harris' Main Force was to attack those Ruhr–Rhineland cities that contained relatively undamaged areas with aiming-point(s) over a railway centre, with two in Bochum and Cologne and one in Dortmund, Duisburg, Essen and Münster. This recommendation indicated some degree of dissatisfaction within the Air Ministry over Harris' choice of aiming-points.

The picturesque Rhineland-Westphalian town of Münster, north of the Ruhr. This target, important for its water and rail communications with the Ruhr, was subjected to an attack by 8 Group on 11–12 June. (Getty Images)

Under pressure, and with its non-operational performances over Germany increasingly under the microscope, Harris finally acted on 11–12 June with a large attack on Düsseldorf and a subsidiary raid on Münster. This was a significant night for the Luftwaffe, in which a new purpose-built night fighter called the He 219 'Uhu' ('Owl') was given its combat debut. With its development having been led by Kammhuber, the machine had high speed, good range, powerful armament and decent visibility from its Perspex cockpit. Like any new aircraft, the He 219 had had its development problems, in particular a violent wobble in its tail at high speeds that was cured by lengthening the fuselage. Nevertheless, in the hands of Werner Streib, now a major with 60 kills, the He 219 prototype made a promising debut by shooting down five bombers in quick succession. However, the success was bittersweet, for the still-untested aircraft was destroyed on landing – the flaps lowered for landing had malfunctioned and retracted back to normal flight – and Streib was lucky to escape serious injury. This set development back several months, but if more efforts had been made to get this aircraft into the hands of Germany's top night-fighter aces, the summer of 1943 may have proven very expensive indeed for Bomber Command. As it was, a PRU sortie some 30 hours later revealed Düsseldorf's fires were still burning, with two square miles of damage in the central area. The Air Ministry Bulletin pronounced that 'much of the damage was done by fire, which evidently swept unchecked over whole districts', suggesting a 'firestorm' had engulfed the city, and described it as 'the most shattering blow' of the Battle of the Ruhr. After many nights of no operations, Harris had needed to deliver a result like this. Bochum was attacked the following night, and Oberhausen on 14–15 June. Both were Musical Wanganui, with sky-markers being sufficiently accurate to do reasonable amounts of damage. Operating in such conditions meant smaller forces,

A Mk.II Halifax of 78 Squadron (EY). The downwards 'blind spot', from which all British heavy bombers remained acutely vulnerable to German night fighter attack, can be seen from this angle. (Tony Buttler Collection)

for only aircraft that could fly above the clouds over the target could go. Thus, on the Bochum attack, the Stirlings were absent, whilst the Oberhausen operation also saw the omission of the Halifaxes. Consequently, the bomber forces sent by Harris from 11–12 to 14–15 June comprised 783, 503 and 203 aircraft respectively.

Bomber Command's lessening efforts were coming under criticism. On 15 June, Churchill was annoyed when Portal informed him that Bomber Command needed a four-day 'lull' in operations so the 'K'-type Oboe and the Monica IFF warning device could be fitted to its aircraft. 'Considering we have just had a "lull" of 13 days in the operations of Bomber Command due to weather,' the prime minister replied, 'it seems a pity that advantage was not taken of this period [to have done this already] … It is rather disappointing now if the weather is going to turn good to stop all the operations.' Describing how June looked like being 'a pretty poor' month for Bomber Command, with the bomb tonnage dropped falling off and the last three attacks showing a rapid decrease in the sizes of the forces sent after the 13-day lull, Churchill was far from impressed, 'considering the enormous claims that are made for the achievements of Bomber Command'. Portal replied the following day, having received an explanation from Harris, citing the weather problems that had forced so many cancelled operations in June. With regards to the small bomber forces used against Bochum and Oberhausen, Portal explained it was 'deemed advisable to send only the [higher-flying] Lancasters'. Thus, he continued, a catch-22 situation had developed, which had served to blunt the bomber offensive and caused Churchill's disappointment:

> Owing to the enormous strength of enemy defences in the Ruhr, he can attack that area in full moonlight only if there is adequate cloud cover. Otherwise he risks heavy and disproportionate losses. If he attacks with cloud cover the flare marker technique restricts the numbers attacking.

Overall, Portal was defending Harris against a serious loss of confidence in the C-in-C on the prime minister's part. He reiterated 'the extreme difficulties' which had confronted Harris and the 'great efforts' he had made to conquer them, adding that decisions affecting the Command's tactical employment had to remain solely the C-in-C's concern. Portal also said he had endorsed the four-day lull. 'I am sure that your comments on the course of these operations do not indicate any lack of confidence in him … to deliver the maximum weight of bombs on Germany with the minimum losses under all conditions,' the CAS concluded. Tellingly, on this minute, Churchill scribbled 'put by'; the benefit-of-the-doubt had been given, but clearly Harris' arguments about Bomber Command on its own winning the war were falling on disbelieving ears.

In the short-term, the effect of Churchill's known unhappiness was that Harris continued to keep Bomber Command operating against the Ruhr, when the lighter nights perhaps should have dictated an alternative approach towards target selection. The casualty figures show these became the grimmest weeks for Bomber Command of the entire campaign, in which the Luftwaffe pilots were increasingly able to find and intercept the British bombers. Bottomley soon raised this issue with Harris. Believing large concentrations of bombers saturated the air defences and lowered the casualty rate, the Air Staff was unhappy that the Dusseldorf raid by nearly 800 aircraft saw losses of five per cent. Harris blamed the bombers' rear turrets, saying they were inadequate to counter night fighters. Meanwhile, the crews engaged in the Battle of the Ruhr would soon find combat with the Luftwaffe night fighters much more intense.

On 12–13 June, the Bomber Command Intelligence Narratives (BCIN) recorded one bomber crew as having seen five Ju 88s around the target area within five minutes. Over Oberhausen, the BCIN noted the night fighter 'was intense', with many combats. A 5 Group Lancaster was attacked by four Ju 88s over the target, with the rear gunner killed, but this aircraft was lucky and got home; 8.4 per cent of the Lancasters did not. On 16–17 June, Bomber Command suffered 6.6 per cent losses as the brilliant moonlight above the clouds over Cologne saw many night fighters waiting to pounce, and such a high level of losses soon became the norm. June's operations to Düsseldorf and Münster, Bochum, Oberhausen, Cologne, Krefeld, Mülheim, Wuppertal-Elberfeld, Gelsenkirchen and Cologne saw the loss of 38 and 5, 24, 17, 14, 44, 35, 34, 30 and 25 aircraft (4.9 per cent and 6.9 per cent, 4.8 per cent, 8.8 per cent, 6.6 per cent, 6.2 per cent, 6.3 per cent, 5.4 per cent, 6.3 per cent and 4.1 per cent) respectively, and a gruesome total of 266 aircraft, roughly a third of Bomber Command's entire front-line strength.[6] Some of the June losses were of experienced crews, not just rookies. On 11–12 June, 467 (RAAF) Squadron's AOC, Sqn Ldr Donald MacKenzie DFC, was shot down on the final operation of his tour, and on board was his successor, Irishman Sqn Ldr Benjamin Ambrose and the squadron's Gunnery Leader, Flt Lt Leslie Betts, their Lancaster a victim of a flak battery some miles east of Aachen. The Krefeld operation saw 7 Squadron lose four Stirlings, two piloted by flight lieutenants, the third flown by a flying-officer and the fourth aircraft containing two squadron leaders, while 24–25 June saw the unit lose another squadron leader and the unit's first Lancaster piloted by Wg Cdr Robert Barrell DSO, DFC & Bar, who suffered the appalling experience of his parachute failing to open. Meanwhile, 35 Squadron had a terrible night on 21–22 June, losing five bombers. These high PFF losses came about because Bennett often overcompensated by sending many more 'backers-up' precisely so an attack would not fail if Oboe had problems. But Main Force units also endured some terrible nights too: 12 Squadron lost five Lancasters on 11–12 June, 427 Squadron four Halifaxes on 22–23 June and 106 Squadron four Lancasters on 25–26 June; 103 Squadron's losses reflected a consistent haemorrhaging rather than a single catastrophic night, with nine Lancasters lost during this month.

Harris later wrote that the Germans 'fully realized' the need to make attacking the Ruhr 'too expensive for us', and the evidence by late June was that the Luftwaffe had almost succeeded. Moreover, the decision taken by Churchill and the service chiefs in May to not use Window, on the rather unconvincing grounds that it would be used by the Luftwaffe in attacks on the UK and the landings in Sicily (Operation *Husky*), looks questionable indeed, especially as they had been informed Window would save 50–60 aircraft during this period.

Bomber Command was, of course, conducting operations against one of the most heavily defended areas in Germany, rich in flak and searchlights thanks to increased production and movement of guns back from northern Italy. One Australian Lancaster pilot recalled how his aircraft was held in a searchlight cone over Cologne for six minutes, in which near misses still put the wireless set out, smashed the electrical panel and blew in the cockpit windows. Cologne became known for having a particularly violent barrage, whilst Gelsenkirchen was notably well defended and was surrounded by the ground defences of the other Ruhr towns. In addition, dangerous target areas were also very crowded – a result of the policy of concentration – which meant the possibility of accidents too. Whilst fatal collisions were rare, a more considerable danger was being struck by bombs dropped from a higher-flying aircraft. On 24–25 June, a Lancaster on its bombing run was struck by an incendiary; fire immediately broke out and the aircraft's metal floor began melting. The bomber was only saved thanks to the endeavours of the bomb aimer who, armed with an axe, began

---

6   By comparison, the 13 attacks on the Ruhr–Rhineland cities from 27–28 January to 30 April–1 May saw a total of 163 bombers missing.

The logistics of the bombing war. A train transporting 4,000lb 'cookie' bombs from their storage at a disused quarry, administered by RAF Maintenance Command, to the front-line bomber squadrons (Getty Images).

hacking away at the burning area and eventually succeeded in releasing the incendiary into the Lancaster's empty bomb bay, from where it then dropped from the aircraft.

Nevertheless, the huge British losses were largely caused by the German night fighters. Partly this was down to the Kammhuber Line working as efficiently as it ever would, and partly to the light nights. The British tactic of concentrating the bomber stream, although vital in helping many aircraft to get through the Kammhuber Line and for overwhelming the defences at the target, meant many bombers could be found in one location, and worse still, they could now be seen. Consequently, some Luftwaffe units would have very successful nights. On 12–13 June, at least ten of the 24 British bombers lost that night were brought down over Holland by III/NJG-1.

In the face of this, the British once again looked at deploying Window, but once again they woefully took the decision to defer its use.

On 25–26 and 28–29 June, the figures were even better for the night fighters, with respectively 21 out of 30 and 20 out of 25 being shot down over the Low Countries. Particularly revealing are the times and location. On 28–29 June, Maj Günther Radusch's four kills were timed approximately at 0212, 0214, 0233 and 0254hrs, all around the Noord Brabant area, whilst the three victories of Schnaufer were around 0130, 0153 and 0155hrs in the vicinity of Liège. This confirms the light conditions were a godsend to night-fighter pilots: GCI was needed for the first interception, but thereafter more bombers could be seen visually and dispatched quickly. If Window had been deployed, then the initial radar detection and GCI control of the German night fighters would have been disrupted, and the June losses would have been less. Bomber Command was paying a high price for the decision to wait to use Window until after Operation *Husky*. Instead, in late June, the Kammhuber Line was left to work very well, whilst its weakness of controlling only one aircraft per box was proving much less of a handicap. One pilot retained communications with the ground, whilst others used aircraft equipped with AI to find bombers within the same area, in a combined GCI and freelance method of night fighting.

That the light nights were allowing the Germans to also follow the bomber stream was confirmed in numerous post-operation British accounts. One aircrew, returned from the Krefeld operation, reported 'more night fighters up than have been encountered for some time, and many combats were reported in the bright moonlight along the route'. Bomber Command's next operation, to Mülheim on 22–23 June, saw many night fighters seen along the route, and the Air Ministry acknowledged that 'during these bright summer nights … every bomber crew expects a battle anywhere over sea or land, coming or going'. The British Bombing Survey Unit (BBSU) noted German tactics were already to place greater numbers of AI-equipped night fighters into the bomber stream on the outward and inbound routes, which made perfect sense given the bombers' illumination in the northern summer sky. In addition, the Luftwaffe seemingly was implementing a further tactical development, one which British aircrews came to actually observe. Back from attacking Gelsenkirchen on 25–26 June, an experienced Australian pilot told post-operation interrogators that 'as we passed through the defence zone both the searchlights and the flak would suddenly cease and then we knew that somewhere a fighter was preparing to attack us'. In fact, the 28–29 June raid saw an intense air battle develop with the Luftwaffe over Cologne:

It was very light about the town – almost like daylight … With the bombers silhouetted against the cloud below, the night fighters had every chance to intercept, and the enemy seemed to have put up as big a force as on any night since the Battle of the Ruhr began.

In this fight, a Polish pilot saw nine combats going on simultaneously, whilst crews from 3 Group reported 14 engagements and, perhaps most tellingly, the German aircraft identified were Fw 190s and Bf 109s. Clearly, the Luftwaffe had added another layer to its fighter defences: using single-engined daytime interceptors for combats over the target area. What the British aircrews were encountering was the German tactic of *Wilde Sau* – German fighters in and around the target area using bright lights from the bombed city, target markers and the glow of fires to pinpoint their target with little need for the radar and GCI Window had jammed. Within weeks it became the standard – and indeed *only* – method of night fighting after Bomber Command was finally allowed to use Window to stem its mounting losses. *Wilde Sau* developed extensively in summer 1943 and included the adoption of radio beacons and a 'running commentary' on the bombers' heading.

To some in the Air Ministry, of course, these casualties only served to underscore the urgent need for Bomber Command to cooperate fully with the Americans in destroying the German fighter aircraft industry. Harris was less keen, however, and prevented (as it stood then) from using Window but facing a revitalized enemy air force, there was no alternative but to continue to battle through to the Ruhr, accepting the large losses of this attritional contest.

Doing so was certainly made more palatable by the heavy blows that Bomber Command was inflicting. The Musical Wanganui attack on Bochum on 12–13 June saw concentrated bombing on accurately placed markers (although one aircraft suffering technical failure dropped its sky markers 12 miles north of the target), and later arrivals saw two large areas of fire in the north and north-east of the city. The same method of attack on 14–15 June against Oberhausen, described by HQ Bomber Command as 'the fifth most important industrial town in the Ruhr' with one of Germany's largest steelworks on a 500-acre site, saw sky markers placed right over the *Altstadt*, which later PRU sorties revealed had been devastated. Lasting just 20 minutes and with 4,000-pounders dropping every 12 seconds, the attack by 705 bombers on Krefeld saw this steel-producing town consumed by one giant raging fire, with smoke three miles high. It appears that a 'firestorm' devastated some 47 per cent of Krefeld's built-up area, in this brutal demonstration of the bombing principle of concentrating an attack in both time and space. Crews attacking Mülheim the following night saw only too clearly Krefeld still burning. Mülheim, yet another of the smaller and largely undamaged Ruhr towns, suffered a similar fate. This was inflicted on a population of 136,000 packed into an urban area smaller than nearby Oberhausen, Bomber Command HQ noted, making it 'one of the most congested towns in the whole district'; this statistic, alongside the town's steel works, coke ovens and railway centre, had contributed to make Mülheim a particularly attractive target for Bomber Command. Reconnaissance photography revealed the extent of the damage, and led to this brutal conclusion from an HQ Bomber Command bulletin to aircrews:

Most of the town of Mülheim stands on the East bank of the River Ruhr, with a few off-shoots on the West Bank. It would be more accurate to say it 'stood' there, for very little on the East bank remains standing.

Krefeld's aesthetically pleasing main railway station. An important railway junction on the west bank of the Rhine, Krefeld was a city of steel production and was attacked by Bomber Command on 21/22 June. Tragically, the indiscriminate nature of area bombing meant beautiful buildings in the Ruhr would also be destroyed. (Getty Images)

It was a massacre. The town centre and 120 acres of residential streets had been flattened, as had the main railway station. Mülheim's two plants of the Verein Stahlwerke, located in the northern and less-damaged part of the town, suffered some destruction. In 1945, the BBSU estimated 64 per cent of the town had been destroyed. But this was all a means to an end. Bomber Command HQ's report on Mülheim shows clearly that they perceived how the breakdown of civilian life impacted on war production. For 'the really significant feature' from the daylight photographs of the two steelworks, they noted, was that:

> In spite of the relatively small amount of material damage revealed, both of them appear to be entirely dead. There is not a sign of normal activity, not a wisp of smoke from the chimneys. It does not necessarily follow that all work in the two factories is entirely at a standstill but the absence of any signs of life is all the more remarkable when it is remembered that these photographs were taken more than a month after the attack.

Clearly, area bombing had caused absenteeism, damage to local transport and reduced supplies of raw materials (such as coal); in other words, the dislocation of a city's transport and public services had obstructed the labour and products needed for Mülheim's war production.

The attack on Mülheim, and Krefeld before it, were part of the campaign against the smaller, steel-producing towns of the Ruhr. One would have expected Hagen to be next, but this was not so. Instead, Harris chose Wuppertal-Elberfeld, which contained the IG Farben Chemical and Pharmaceutical Works and the Jaeger Ball-Bearing Factory (part of a target system that included the plants at Schweinfurt), and Bomber Command once more found its mark. Several fires took hold around the aiming-point, which soon merged into one large conflagration that quickly overwhelmed the firefighters. Although there was some scattered bombing, with some creepback and 30 aircraft dropping their bombs in the wrong part of the Ruhr, the BBSU estimated that 94 per cent of Elberfeld was destroyed in this attack. June's final attack was on Cologne, the second of four operations against this city during a period of three weeks. In 10/10 cloud, the accuracy of the sky marking eventually allowed Bomber Command to deliver its heaviest blow of the campaign, which Cologne felt as its worst night of the war. Fires, smoke columns and explosions in the southern suburbs were seen by aircrews for miles, and a particularly large detonation 'turned the sky scarlet' for some time. Thus ended a costly month in which Bomber Command's huge losses had been exchanged for inflicting considerable, if far from complete, devastation on a number of cities in the Ruhr–Rhineland.

Endgame: the attacks of July

By early July, the German night-fighter pilots could feel pleased with the number of British bombers they had recently shot down, and their successes continued into the new month. The Cologne operation of 3–4 July is generally regarded as the first sign the Luftwaffe was making attacks over the targets, although clearly this had been attempted previously. One aircrew experienced a night fighter following them many miles to the target, which indicated the Luftwaffe was ascertaining the precise target so its single-engined fighters could be sent to intercept. These 'freelancing' aircraft depended on the illumination in the target area from searchlights, target-markers and ground fires to see the outline of the British bombers from above. At this stage, the success of *Wilde Sau* should not be exaggerated, with only seven Bf 109s and five Fw 190s allocated. Nonetheless, this method deployed on 8–9 July left an impression on the British. 'Many,' the Air Ministry Bulletin stated, 'were hotly engaged when actually over Cologne … when their pilots had a good chance of spotting the bombers silhouetted against the red glow of fires or the diffused light of the searchlights on the cloud.' Some night fighters, at great risk to themselves, attacked the British bombers over the target even when the heavy flak was in full barrage.

Despite the increasingly hot target areas, the 13–14 July operation to Aachen still saw the majority of losses (12 from 20 aircraft) over northern France, Belgium, Holland and Luxembourg. This operation was Bomber Command's last attack of the Battle of the Ruhr in the pre-Window era, and the urgent need for introducing this radar counter-measure was now compelling. Following the *Husky* landings in Sicily, Churchill and the Chiefs of Staff Committee finally sanctioned its use after 23 July. Though first used against Hamburg, it would be deployed on the final two attacks of the Ruhr air campaign, against Essen on 24–25 July and Remscheid on 30–31 July.

Blinding the Würzburg radars, Window was used alongside other counter-measures that saw Mandrel interfere with the Freya early-warning radars, Tinsel the radio communications between ground controller and German pilot, and Grocer with the night fighter's AI equipment. The 25–26 July operation to Essen saw only 3.7 per cent (26 aircraft) lost, with the majority being over the Ruhr, not over the Low Countries. Only the experienced Streib secured his four victories in the skies over Holland. Streib's successes indicated that, although the Kammhuber Line had been neutralized, the skill of a night-fighter ace in using the light summer sky could still be rewarded. The attack on Remscheid on 30–31 July saw 15 aircraft lost, but this equated to 5.5 per cent of the small bomber force despatched. This was high, but was probably due to the force comprising mostly of Bomber Command's outdated aircraft, the Halifax II/V and Stirling, with five and eight missing respectively. The Stirling's 9.2 per cent casualty rate was, Webster and Frankland assert, because this slower aircraft fell behind and therefore did not receive the full protection of Window by being packed into the bomber stream. This was certainly plausible, but it was equally apparent that this aircraft's service over Germany was almost up.

The attack on Essen on 25–26 July was by 705 bombers, and notable for over 2,000 tons of bombs being dropped. These figures show how, despite the losses, Bomber Command's destructive capabilities had risen during the campaign, for the attack on 5–6 March had seen 442 bombers drop 1,054 tons of bombs on Essen. The July attack was deliberately staged so that Window could be exploited to deliver the *coup de grâce* on Essen; the earlier raids had been destructive, but enough industrial activity had remained for Essen to maintain its position as a high-priority target. The subsequent bombing was colossal, and achieved its objective of devastating the Krupp Works and the industrial areas in the eastern suburbs. Essen became a scene of violent explosions, thick smoke plumes up to 22,000ft and fires so vast that the glow could be seen by British rear gunners when back over the Dutch coast. Goebbels recorded that the attack had 'caused a complete stoppage of production in the Krupps works', which made Speer 'much concerned and worried'.

British success was due to an expansion of Oboe stations. It must be remembered that Oboe's control of one aircraft every five minutes, together with only two pairs of stations operating, had on some Ruhr attacks caused 'gaps' to appear in the marking, which were often compounded by the not infrequent malfunctions of the Oboe equipment itself. Thus, when a force of over 700 bombers was sent and took 40–50 minutes to complete the marking, the continuity of marking throughout the attack could become very marginal indeed. This problem, coupled with ground-markers simply becoming unsighted or sky-markers drifting away, had often caused the bombing to become less concentrated. However, this was not the case on 25–26 July, because a third pair of Oboe ground stations had become operable; in addition, a third Oboe channel was introduced. The net effect was that more marker aircraft could be controlled, which meant the marking could be renewed more continuously, and was just as accurate for the last bombing wave as it was for the first. The damage was sufficiently

The Commander-in-Chief Bomber Command, Air Chief-Marshal Sir Arthur Harris. The photograph was taken on 10 July 1943, towards the end of the air campaign against the Ruhr, for the publication *Picture Post*. The previous night Harris' bombers had made an unsuccessful attack against Gelsenkirchen. (Getty Images)

The Rhineland city of Cologne, with its distinctive twin-spired cathedral. Towards the end of the Battle of the Ruhr, Harris focused on destroying this important industrial and transportation centre on the Rhine. He no doubt endeavoured to show Britain's war leaders that a smaller number of four-engined bombers, especially Lancasters, could drop as many bombs as that dropped by the Thousand-Bomber Force of mixed-aircraft types in June 1942. (Getty Images)

complete that Essen would not receive another major attack until 26–27 March 1944.

In these last weeks of the Ruhr campaign, there was a significant focus on Cologne, which was attacked repeatedly because it was Germany's third largest city and considered by Bomber Command HQ to be 'the industrial centre of the Rhineland'. Whilst smaller places, like Wuppertal or Krefeld, had only one aiming-point to bring about their destruction, Cologne had four. Having been attacked on 16–17 June and 28–29 June, it was targeted again on 3–4 July and 8–9 July. With crews able to see the Rhine and the bridges across it owing to good visibility, the Oboe ground-marking on the aiming-point on the Rhine's east bank saw bombs and large fires break out in Cologne's major industrial areas of Kalk and Deutz, which bordered Mülheim.[7] Together, these three areas were considered by Bomber Command HQ as especially important, for they formed a congested and compact industrial area of five square miles, with many industrial workers, numerous factories and extensive railways. Several days later, Goebbels himself arrived to assess the situation, and if he stayed the night he would have witnessed the raid on 8–9 July. Although a poor weather forecast limited the effort to just 282 Lancasters and six Mosquitoes, the 9–10–10 cloud cover from 10,000–17,000ft over Cologne saw the Musical Wanganui method mark the aiming-point, this time located west of the river. Faults with Oboe delayed and scattered the initial marking, but a generous supply of sky-markers dropped after 0014hrs brought concentrated damage to the north-western and south-western parts of the city. In the aftermath, Harris ordered full photographic coverage of Cologne, which revealed three-quarters of the built-up area damaged, severe destruction to the city centre and considerable devastation in the industrial districts on the east bank. The final part of the campaign had been marked by a particularly concentrated assault against one major city, and it might be said that a 'Battle of Cologne' was the precursor to the one soon launched against Hamburg.

Destruction was, however, brought to new targets, Aachen and Remscheid, places that Harris later described as 'subsidiary outlying towns' (like Wuppertal, Remscheid, Krefeld, Münster and Mönchengladbach), attacked once the Ruhr's 'core' industrial centres had been heavily bombed. Lying some miles south of the Ruhr, Remscheid had a population of 107,000 and contained two industries that used 'special steel' to make aero-engine crankshafts and machine tools. Aachen, on the other hand, had several small, insignificant factories, but was an important railway centre. It seems that purely tactical considerations motivated Bomber Command to attack these two towns according to the HQ Bomber Command bulletin to aircrews:

'preventing the removal of defences to other threatened areas' from the Ruhr, and equally importantly, discouraging the return of industrial workers from other parts of Germany. Middlebrook cites German records describing the Aachen attack as purely a '*Terrorangriff*' ('terror attack', and Bomber Command's own Quarterly Review certainly hinted at this:

The attacks on Aachen and Remscheid had a different kind of importance. Following as they did on the annihilation of Wuppertal and Krefeld, they drove home the lesson that a single successful attack can write off an industrial city of considerable size and value in a single night. Recognition of this important fact has had a stimulating effect on the evacuation of similar towns in Western Germany to the disadvantage of war production and administration.

7   A district of Cologne, not to be confused with the Ruhr town.

What this amounted to was terrorizing the inhabitants of any small town in western Germany into believing that, quite literally, nowhere was safe. Aachen was bombed by 374 aircraft, which contained no Main Force Lancasters (these had just made the very long trip to Turin), but the Halifaxes, Stirlings and Wellingtons remained sufficient to overwhelm the local fire brigade and cause a widespread conflagration that devastated half the town. Indeed, unlike other Ruhr targets where the ratio of HEs to IBs had been around 2:1, the attacks on Aachen saw it reversed, with the bombload consisting of 545.5 tons of incendiaries and 329.1 tons HE. Remscheid's proportion was similar, carried by a force of 273 aircraft – those from 1 and 5 Groups remained on standby for bombing Italy – which found good visibility over the target and it only lightly defended, leading to another destructive attack. Conceived as a joint attack with Solingen, the 778.4 tons of bombs – with 62 per cent IBs – dropped on Remscheid proved enough: later reconnaissance photographs showed the devastation was vast, the BBSU assessing that fire had consumed 83 per cent of Remscheid, with about 8,000 people killed or injured, and 107 industrial buildings and 3,115 dwellings destroyed. Such was the devastating – and brutal – outcome of area bombing on small targets, which was what its practitioners intended. Remscheid had thus joined Aachen, Düsseldorf-Derendorf, Krefeld, Mülheim and Wuppertal-Elberfeld, where, to use German historian Jörg Heinrich's book title, *Der Brand* ('The Fire') from Bomber Command attacks had inflicted colossal damage during June and July 1943.

Bomber Command's only disappointment during this time was Gelsenkirchen, notoriously difficult to locate and brutally defended by the guns throughout the Ruhr. The Air Ministry noted that on 9–10 July, 'German defences put up one of the fiercest barrages since the Battle of the Ruhr began … which opened up as soon as the bombers entered the Ruhr area, until the barrage spread over an area that could be measured in miles'. Within this, the sheer amount of flak exploding beneath one Lancaster twice blew it onto its back. This ferocious barrage defended Gelsenkirchen's sprawling area of coal mines, steelworks, marshalling yards and railway lines, and particularly two of the largest synthetic oil plants in German-occupied Europe. This seemed an opportunity for Harris to show that specific plants could be damaged by an area raid rather than by a precision attack. Alas, two attacks on Gelsenkirchen on 25–26 June and 9–10 July 1943 saw Bomber Command lose 42 aircraft for very little damage inflicted. The first attack's sky-marking was all but ruined by Oboe failures; only four of nine Mosquitoes marked the target, and later waves of Main Force aircraft saw no sky-markers and simply dropped their bombs on the glow of fires through 10/10 cloud. Similar target conditions pertained on 9–10 July, when things were even worse as five Mosquitoes could not drop their sky-markers due to problems with Oboe, while the sixth dropped its markers ten miles away. Such a complete disaster suggests the Germans were jamming the system. Fires and explosions indicated that *something* had been hit, but most of the bombs fell in neighbouring Bochum and Wattenscheid.

For Bomber Command, the Battle of the Ruhr ended after five months of attrition that had delivered some gains, although they were far from clear. But in Harris' mind, it was just the first step towards achieving victory through bombing, in which a land campaign on the Continent would be rendered unnecessary. In the end, that understandable aim, of avoiding vast casualties on the ground, had been substituted by carnage in the air as an 'aerial Passchendaele' had taken place in the skies over north-west Europe from March–July 1943.

A damaged Lancaster from 106 Squadron, crash-landed at its home base of Syerston, owing to attack by a German night fighter. Many more such casualties would follow during the Battle of the Ruhr. (© IWM CE 3)

AFTERMATH AND ANALYSIS

A Lancaster over the Ruhr showing the destructive power of an area attack by Bomber Command. This picture was probably taken in spring 1945 during the 'Third Battle of the Ruhr' as Harris was by then sending his bomber force on daylight attacks against this area. (Getty Images)

It is questionable when the Ruhr campaign ended, and why. Clearly, there was a conscious decision to move away from the Ruhr in summer 1943. From 12–13 July, Bomber Command was asked to undertake operations supporting Operation *Husky*, and bombed Turin that night. The *British Official History* regarded Aachen on 13–14 July as the campaign's last action, 'if only' because next would be Hamburg. This author agrees with Saward and Richards that the Remscheid operation on 30–31 July marked its end. Yet despite its successes, the campaign had been costly for Bomber Command, to the point where it was becoming potentially unviable.

If only including the Ruhr/Rhineland attacks, then 720 bombers were lost; if the entire campaign's 43 operations are considered, then 872 aircraft were missing, which of course encompasses the 36 bombers (11 per cent) lost on the first Pilsen operation – the costliest attack of the entire battle. Behind these overall totals lay some grim operational statistics, especially for the attacks undertaken in June against Oberhausen (8.4 per cent losses), Cologne (14.4 per cent), Krefeld (6.2 per cent), Mülheim (6.3 per cent) and Gelsenkirchen (6.3 per cent). The least expensive were the attacks on Duisburg on 26–27 March (1.2 per cent) and 26–27 April (3.0 per cent). But taken as a whole, Bomber Command lost around 4.8 per cent of aircraft on Ruhr operations, which as the *British Official History* states 'were grave losses and [meant] the margin left to Bomber Command with which to preserve the future fighting efficiency of the force was narrow indeed'. Indeed, towards the end of war, Sydney Bufton wrote a paper that specifically examined this issue. He concluded that wartime experience had shown:

> A strategic bomber force would become relatively ineffective if it suffered operational losses in the region of 7% over a period of 3 months' intensive operations, and that its operational effectiveness may become unacceptably low if losses of 5% were sustained over this period

Moreover, at squadron level, 'The Reaper' had been busy cutting a swathe through Bomber Command's ranks, especially among the Halifax operators of 76, 77 and 78 Squadrons, and in 7 Squadron, the Pathfinders' Stirling unit, which lost aircraft in most attacks. Yet, as Sydney Bufton writes, figures 'do not show the strain which was imposed upon the resilient morale of the Bomber Command aircrews, nor do they reveal the extent to which the force suffered from the loss of many experienced men who might have become leaders on other operations or instructors at Operational Training Units'. This, coupled with the colossal number of aircraft returning damaged – some of which could be unserviceable for weeks while being repaired – clearly indicated that a change of target was becoming highly desirable.

There was also the background consideration of a new focus in Anglo–American bombing policy, a consequence of the Combined Chiefs of Staff meeting

The I.G. Farben chemical works at Leverkusen, a city on the Rhine lying between Düsseldorf and Cologne. This target was attacked on 22–23 August and 19–20 November 1943, but both raids did little damage. (Getty Images)

during the Washington Conference in May. The Pointblank Directive, issued on 10 June, stipulated an increased effort against German aircraft production, but Bomber Command's primary objective of German industry and morale meant Harris moved away from the Ruhr to Germany's second largest city, Hamburg. Bomber Command HQ sent the Bomber Groups the operation order for Operation *Gomorrah*, the destruction of Hamburg, on 27 May. Enshrined in the operation order was Harris' justification for doing so in terms of following the Casablanca Directive. With a population of 1.1 million, it was stated, 'the total destruction of this city would achieve immeasurable results in reducing the industrial capacity of the enemy's war machine', with the effect on morale being felt throughout Germany.

Yet, for the rest of 1943, Bomber Command would not be finished with the Ruhr. After 31 July, the Air Staff wanted Harris to continue to bomb this area, but designed to fulfil more specific purposes, such as rail and water transportation. For example, 617 Squadron was to attack shiplifts, canal embankments, locks and river barrages along the Dortmund–Ems and Mittelland Canals (this being done from autumn 1943). Cutting rail communications through the Ruhr saw attacks made on Leverkusen (22–23 August and 19–20 November), Mönchengladbach/Rheydt (30–31 August), Bochum (29–30 September), Hagen (1–2 October) and Düsseldorf/Cologne (3–4 November) precisely because they contained untouched or relatively undamaged built-up areas, with sizeable populations, which had aiming-points over a railway station or marshalling yard.

Major raids were flown to disrupt industrial reconstruction and target undamaged industries such as IG Farben's chemical works in Leverkusen. The twin towns of were known for clothing and textiles; 'shortage of these products in Germany is already so acute,' the MEW assessed, 'that provision of new clothes and other textile goods is practically limited to the armed forces and the bombed-out. The consequences of any further limitation of supplies may therefore be very serious both at home and at the fronts.' This showed the wider consideration about bombing industries and its impact on civilian morale, and

Set in a valley on the south-eastern outskirts of the Ruhr was the town of Hagen, which was attacked on 1–2 October 1943 causing considerable damage to the town's Accumulator Factory and residential districts. (Getty Images)

the attack on Mönchengladbach/Rheydt would be especially large, given the modest size of the target, involving 660 aircraft.

Bomber Command attacked the 'special steel'-producing plants of Vereinigte Stahlwerke in Bochum on 29–30 September, and followed this up by bombing the other centre producing this type of steel, Hagen, which also contained the very important target of Accumulatoren-Fabrik Co (Class 1+) making batteries for U-boats. Düsseldorf's war industries were targeted by 589 aircraft dropping 2,100 tons of bombs in just 27 minutes, which included 38 Lancaster Mk IIs from 3 and 6 Groups using the new G-H blind-bombing device to bomb the Mannesmannröhrenwerke in its northern outskirts; this represented the last major operation against the Ruhr–Rhineland for 1943, although small Mosquito nuisance raids against this area continued throughout the forthcoming winter.

In essence, there was a feeling at Bomber Command HQ that it had 'done the job' against the Ruhr, with the 58,000 tons of bombs dropped during the air campaign having brought the German people face-to-face with the grim reality of total war. Indeed, on 3 November, Harris informed Churchill that with regards to the Ruhr, only attacks on Solingen, Witten and Leverkusen needed to be made, as well as to 'tidy up all round when occasion serves'; he told Major-General Ira Eaker, commander of the US Eighth Air Force, the following day that this also included Gelsenkirchen and Hamm, and to 'revisit other targets when occasion offers to prevent rehabilitation and retain defences'. The destruction inflicted meant Harris now classified the Ruhr as the ninth and lowest priority. But was the C-in-C correct in informing the prime minister that the Ruhr was now 'largely "out"'? Certainly, Harris' memorandum had itself set the yardstick by which the Battle of the Ruhr can be judged.

It must be said Harris had a definite agenda in sending this memorandum, to secure prime ministerial support for the Battle of Berlin in the face of doubters within the Air Ministry and also to gain Churchill's help in getting the US Eighth to join in. By its very nature, therefore, the claims on Bomber Command's previous area bombing campaigns were going to be bold, if not highly exaggerated. But the key problem was what evidence could be used to make such claims about the levels of destruction in the Ruhr and Hamburg. The indicator given to foreign statesmen, as well as to the Press, was the 'acreage destroyed' figure, which represented the crude notion that areas of vast devastation could not possibly function in either an industrial or civil sense.

On 3 September 1943, Harris and his wife attended an exhibition organized by the *Daily Express* called the 'Path to Victory', whose centrepiece exhibit was a model of blitzed Essen. The obsession with physical devastation as *the* indicator of bombing's success was readily apparent, and even after the war, Harris wrote that the Ruhr–Rhineland cities were 'in most instances heavily damaged, the devastated areas amounting to hundreds and in some instances to thousands of acres, usually right in the centre of the city'. Within this widespread devastation, he claimed, industrial production had suffered considerably: Essen saw a 30 per cent reduction, with the output of locomotives and fuses ceasing in March 1943, large shells stopping in July, and armoured gun turrets and aircraft engine crankshafts declining from this point. May 1943 marked a turning point downwards of Bochum's coal and steel production, which averaged out to 55 per cent of their pre-raid level. The two large attacks on Dortmund in May 1943 marked the start of a longer-term 30 per cent reduction, which accelerated after

Strategic bombing's dreadful cost: dead civilians lying in a Bochum street, probably victims of the heavy British attack on 29–30 September 1943. (Getty Images)

Joseph Goebbels, Reich Minister of Propaganda and Gauleiter of Berlin, addressing the party faithful in Dortmund in mid-June 1943. Dortmund was hit hard during the Battle of the Ruhr and subjected to the largest attack of the entire air campaign (826 aircraft on 23–24 May). Unlike Hitler, Goebbels visited the Ruhr several times during spring 1943 to organize relief efforts. He frequently described the devastation he witnessed in his diary, including that to his hometown of Mönchengladbach/ Rheydt as a consequence of Bomber Command's attack on 30–31 August 1943. (Getty Images)

autumn 1944 following several huge attacks. But Harris' greatest claim about the Battle of the Ruhr was its effect on Düsseldorf, with the raids of May and June 1943 causing an average reduction in production of 70 per cent. Harris probably based this on the estimate of RE8 (a branch of the MoHS), which the *British Official History* later described as 'much too high' because Düsseldorf's industries lay on its outskirts and were hardly affected. In fact, RE8's assessment of the bombing's impact on Germany's capacity to make war, which would be accepted by the Air Ministry and the Americans, was just some 9–15 per cent loss in war production in the period from March to December 1943. Like Harris, RE8 also made its judgements based on analysis of aerial photographs of the bombed targets, with assumptions then drawn about the level of production and the devastation shown. Indeed, on 19 October 1943, the MoHS produced a report on the effects of Bomber Command's attacks on German cities from 4 July to 30 September, which attempted to form some basis of calculation based on a three-step formula: acres damaged = houses damaged = working hours lost. Figures were calculated for the first two categories, which led to the conclusion that 'on the basis of a rough estimate of the number of industrial workers in the bombed towns, it appears that on the average all towns together lost some 3 weeks' production', with the greater destruction to Remscheid (and Hamburg) seeing an 11-week loss. But the MoHS report ultimately contained two key words: 'rough estimate'. In fairness, during wartime, there were few alternative ways of ascertaining the effect bombing was having on German war production. Moreover, a considerable flaw was failure to fully appreciate that factories which showed external damage could still, and often did, have working machinery inside them. The United States Strategic Bombing Survey (USSBS) survey of the Krupp Works, for example, showed how American and British wartime analysts had 'not realized that even when the roofs and other parts of buildings had been destroyed the heavy machinery remained intact and production would soon be resumed'.[8] Harris later

8   For industrial targets, a mass of incendiaries was better, for these fell into the roofless factories, causing an intense conflagration that damaged plant machinery beyond repair, often by melting its parts and burning its lubricants. Bomber Command seemed to overlook this fact during the Battle of the Ruhr, however.

wrote that 'the wrecked cities of the Ruhr' still needed to be 'attacked once or even twice again to prevent recovery'. Unlike the Battle of Hamburg, which after all was against one city, the Ruhr campaign could never be a short engagement owing to the sheer multitude of targets. Added to cancellations caused by the weather, it was little wonder it soon stretched out over five months. Herein lay the problem, for this allowed the Ruhr's cities time to recover, with organized labour battalions mobilized to clear rubble and repair plant and machinery. The critique of Harris' post-war Despatch by the Air Staff, hardly a neutral source it must be said, highlighted this limitation: 'Figures can be adduced to show that the attacks on cities failed to produce conclusive results because, in view of the recovery factor (the Germans' recuperative powers were remarkable), the tempo of the attacks was unavoidably too slow.' This allowed the restoration of industrial production to near its pre-raid level within months, if not sooner. Even during the war, the MEW had noted that, for all the 'extremely severe damage' inflicted on Essen by July 1943, intense reconstruction efforts allowed industrial production to recover 40 per cent of its pre-raid figure by the year's end.

TOWN	PERCENTAGE OF SERIOUSLY DAMAGED BUILDINGS					PERCENTAGE OF SERIOUSLY DAMAGED HOUSING
	All buildings	Industrial buildings	Non-industrial buildings	All buildings		
				Within Zones 1 and 2	Within Zones 4 and 5	
Damage exceeding 50 per cent						
Kassel	54	37	62	78	39	54
Remscheid	53	38	59	96	40	51
Hamburg	51	32	60	73	33	56
Damage 25–50 per cent						
Düsseldorf	41	32	46	68	26	36
Cologne	40	27	46	52	29	32
Mönchengladbach	37	22	46	72	20	47
Aachen	33	23	39	50	14	42
Wuppertal-Barmen	33	16	41	66	21	37
Wuppertal-Elberfeld	32	24	35	66	23	35
Krefeld	25	16	29	48	8	30
Damage 10–25 per cent						
Mülheim	23	14	27	76	15	23
Essen	20	28	16	27	41	24
Dortmund	19	22	17	36	18	20
Bochum	17	13	20	48	16	19
Hagen	15	9	20	37	8	16
Oberhausen	10	5	14	2	3	15
Damage less than 10 per cent						
Duisburg	8	6	10	14	5	9
Münster	5	6	5	5	9	4

Ascertaining the reality could be achieved, it was hoped, by analyzing the conditions on the ground, specifically German evidence. Consequently, in summer 1945, survey teams from America and Britain set out for Germany to determine the effect of strategic bombing on the Nazi war economy. However, the USSBS got its conclusions out first – focusing on late 1944 when American daylight bombers targeted Ruhr steel.

Overall, the USSBS concluded that area attacks on the Ruhr only caused a 2.5 per cent loss of production in 1942, 9.0 per cent in 1943 and 17.0 per cent in 1944. What had really broken the German war machine, according to the Americans, was their precision targeting of specific industries. Such a conclusion seemed partly based on information given by Speer after the war, which seemed to be telling his American interrogators what they wanted to hear about their bombing philosophy. Contradicting his wartime message, such as the speech on 23 June 1943 that acknowledged Bomber Command 'was hitting the right target', Speer stated that the effect of Bomber Command's night attacks 'on industry were very slight' and that 'area bombing alone would never have been a serious threat'. Instead, it was the daylight attacks on Schweinfurt that caused 'a renewed crisis', and thus 'mass attacks by day' on specific industries were far more effective in weakening German war production than area attacks by night. In

Duisburg was a vital area of heavy industry and transportation centre. At Ruhrort, north of the River Ruhr, it contained one of the largest inland ports in Europe. This picture shows the devastation to this area by April 1945. (Getty Images)

addition, the USSBS argued that Krupps – arguably the British obsession when it came to targets in the Ruhr – was no longer engaged in mass war production and had, by spring 1943, become more a 'centre of development'. In contrast, the BBSU took a more nuanced view, looking at how area bombing had either affected war production directly, through damage to factories, or indirectly, through disruption to public utilities (electricity, water, telephone), local transport, labour absenteeism, workers transferred to rubble clearance and reconstruction, shortages of raw materials or dispersal of plant machinery.[9] Consequently, the BBSU undertook, according to Professor Richard Overy, 'a more detailed enquiry into the effects which area attacks on Germans towns had on production in each defined group of industries in the Reich'. Whilst utilizing the USSBS reports, the British team prepared their own research material, which included individual studies of 20 industrial towns, employee questionnaires on production and damage, German statistics and documents from those who had been directly responsible for industry and war production. Yet notwithstanding the more forensic approach, which was as thorough as it could be, the conclusions drawn could hardly be definite, although they correlated quite closely with the assessments made during the war. The British team also interviewed senior German officials. Speer said the impact on German war production from bombing the Ruhr was felt much later, from September 1944, when attacks on the Reichsbahn (the German railway system) affected the movement of the region's coal supplies. The Head of the Armaments Supply Office, Walter Schieber, stated that air attacks from spring 1942 to summer 1944 'were not able to reduce Ruhr output to any great extent', which 'reached its maximum in Autumn '43 and spring of '44 but would have been greater still but for bombing'. Walther Rohland, chairman of the Main Committee for the Iron Producing Industry, said that the effect on Ruhr production 'would have been more serious if the attacks had been sustained'. At best, the BBSU 'estimated' – often the most critical word frequently used – there was two to two-and-a-half months' loss of production up to November 1943.

9   The *USSBS* survey found Solingen to be 'an example of how a town not hit itself suffered from the destruction of others for many of its workers lived in Wuppertal and Remscheid', whilst Rheinmetall-Borsig in Düsseldorf 'shows what dispersal might do, since its machinery, sent away to save it from destruction, was never used again during the war'.

In spring 1945, even before the war ended, Bomber Command HQ itself recognized that 'the effects of attacks upon industrial centres are obviously much less easy to assess than those of attacks upon individual targets and target systems'. One target system was, of course, workers' morale and productivity. During the war, this was very difficult to ascertain. The *Sicherheitsdienst* (SD, the Security Service) did monitor the German population after air raids, but the British hardly had access to this information. British intelligence did receive reports from 'neutrals', particularly Swedish businessmen, on conditions inside Germany, but these tended to relate to Berlin rather than the Ruhr. On 18 July 1945, specifically responding to a question on the 'the willingness and ability of the civilian population to sustain the war effort', Speer told his interrogators:

> We drew distinction between morale and conduct. *The morale following attacks upon towns was bad, the conduct of the civil population on the other hand was admirable* [original emphasis].

'Conduct', he continued, was measured by such things as war production output and 'the will to rebuild the factories', and this never collapsed during the Battle of the Ruhr and in fact remained 'unimpaired right up to the end'. German historian Götz Bergander, a young man in Dresden during the war, claims a distinction existed between 'private morale' and 'war morale', in which the former – entwined with notions of an individual and family's survival and future – was never broken. In contrast, Bergander asserted:

> The air raids on cities and industry shook the foundations of the war morale of the German people. They permanently shattered their nerves, undermined their health and shook their belief in victory … They spread fear, dismay, and hopelessness. This was an important and intentional result of the strategic air war.

What did this amount to in the Battle of the Ruhr? Recent scholarship has added to our understanding by showing that heavy attacks on the region certainly caused the German authorities to become worried about shaken morale. As early as mid-April 1943, the Reich Interior Ministry issue a relocation order (*Umquartierung*) for the Ruhr's industrial workers to be accommodated in other parts of the Rhineland, and for non-essential civilians – such as children and the elderly – to be sent to more distant and rural areas.

So what was the Battle of the Ruhr's effect on the production of certain basic commodities, such as steel, which was after all one of the key products produced in the area? The BBSU noted:

> German war production was always potentially threatened … It is not until we come to the first half of 1944 that indications can be found that production programmes were reaching the ceiling set by the limitation of certain basic supplies, and of steel in particular … [However,] the evidence is that even up to the spring of 1944 the output of ordinary steel was sufficient, not only for a 50 per cent expansion in production for the Wehrmacht, but also for the provision of 300,000 tons of steel monthly for use in the civilian sector of production.

Thus, as the *British Official History* concludes, 'on the whole there was little illusion as to the small effect produced' by Bomber Command's Battle of the Ruhr. However, recent work by one expert on the Nazi war economy suggests Bomber Command's attacks on the Ruhr's steel output proved more significant. Adam Tooze writes that 'following the onset of heavy air raids in the first quarter of 1943, steel production fell by 200,000 tons … All the painstaking effort that had gone into reorganizing the rationing system [of steel output] was negated by the ability of the British to disrupt production more or less at will.' Indeed, this steel shortage caused Hitler and Speer, following a long discussion between 13 and 15 May, to 'implement an immediate cut to the ammunition programme' that meant ordnance production increased by only 20 per cent in 1943, in contrast to 1942 when it had doubled. Yet viewed from another angle, statistics were acquired on the number of railway wagons required for the transportation of steel and coal to Germany's other industrial centres. The British had, of course, identified the Ruhr's railway system as a vulnerable point liable to disruption from bombing. Between January–March 1943 and January–March 1944, the wagon allocation remained at the high level of 20,000, and showed only a very substantial decrease in January 1945 to 9,500, after the Ruhr's marshalling yards had been badly hit during the 'Second Battle of the Ruhr' undertaken the previous autumn. This caused Speer to become seriously concerned that supplies of raw materials were becoming bottled up in the Ruhr, but this had not been the case with the earlier campaign against the Ruhr in 1943. However, once again, the position was rather more complicated. A separate team of the BBSU, which was specifically dedicated to examining the effect of strategic bombing on Germany's inland communications, identified August 1943 as 'the first significant crisis', in which wagons needed by agricultural areas for transporting the grain and root harvests 'could not be satisfied' owing to their urgent need elsewhere following bombing attacks on Essen, Duisburg and Dortmund.

Certainly, the Battle of the Ruhr came at the time when Germany's economy needed to be geared towards a more intensified war effort, not least to support the Wehrmacht's increasingly desperate battle of attrition in Russia, and it must be remembered that only weeks before the British air campaign had commenced, Goebbels had given the battle cry for 'total war' mobilization. This critical moment in Germany's strategic fortunes during spring 1943 was exactly the time when, as Tooze correctly observes, 'the German war economy itself was sucked directly in the fighting … the Ruhr was raised from the status of the home front to that of a war zone'. Thus, the 34,000 tons of bombs dropped on the Ruhr by Bomber Command in 1943 'struck against the most vital node of the German industrial economy' and occurred precisely at the time when Hitler and Speer hoped 'to energize armaments production', especially to replace the huge losses of tanks; the Ostheer (the German army in the East) possessed only 495 tanks in the aftermath of Stalingrad, not all being operable. With arms production heavily reliant on the Ruhr's steel production, Bomber Command seemed to be hitting the right place at the right time, with destruction in the Ruhr by implication adversely affecting German military power. Thus, argues Tooze, 'there can be no doubt that the Battle of the Ruhr marked a turning point in the history of the German war economy, which has been grossly underestimated by post-war accounts'. However, the BBSU, clearly predisposed towards praising the attack on Germany's oil and transportation system, had stated that the area attacks on Germany's industrial cities before early 1944 'had only an irritant effect on German production'. Webster and Frankland concluded that 'the results were important, but in no

The colossal damage inflicted on the Ruhr by 1945. Notwithstanding the air campaign of 1943, the region's towns and cities remained consistent targets for RAF Bomber Command right up to the end of the war. (Getty Images)

sense crippling and small in comparison with the general rise of armament production at the time'. Tooze, taking a much broader view, writes how 'disrupting production in the Ruhr had the capacity to halt assembly lines across Germany', such as in Berlin; as a result, production problems caused by attacks on the Ruhr meant summer 1943 saw the *Zulieferungkrise* (sub-component crisis), with many parts, castings and forgings 'suddenly in short supply', affecting 'not only heavy industry directly, but the entire armament complex'. For example, shortages of the 'special steel' produced in the Ruhr for manufacturing crankshafts for aero-engines brought 'the rapid increase in Luftwaffe production to an abrupt halt'.

Elsewhere, Bomber Command's raids did see direct hits, which it would be churlish to call 'lucky', on factories producing vital components. The Cologne operation of 3–4 July saw damage inflicted on the Humbold-Deutz factory making U-boat accumulators, and because of this, according to a BBSU report, 'supplies from this area for U-boat construction could not be maintained'. Speer's interrogation on 18 July 1945 saw him mention U-boat production being considerably affected by the attack on Hagen, which saw severe damage to the plant making batteries.

Speer's speech to the Nazi Gauleiters of June 1943 was thus an acknowledgement, Tooze argues, that Bomber Command's attacks 'had negated all plans for a further increase in production … [and] had stopped Speer's armaments miracle in its tracks', which was heightened by the colossal losses sustained in Russia and the Eastern Front's clear descent into a battle of attrition involving the mass production of weaponry. Bomber Command's attacks on the Ruhr had curtailed increases in arms production, which fell from the planned 15–20 per cent to only about 3–5 per cent, which was 'absolutely insufficient', Speer stated. Yet the Reich Minister of Armaments and War Production was 'over-optimistic' in this assessment, for 'the monthly index of armaments showed no consistent increase whatsoever in the second half of 1943'. Tooze therefore offers a more definite view than the official historians, who ascribe the stagnation in German war production during late 1943 as partly being a result of the Battle of the Ruhr but also being 'more to other causes'. He even argues that 'the failure' to maintain the aerial pressure on the Ruhr and even 'tighten it' was 'a tragic operational error'[10] – although to have done so may have been unwise tactically.

Overy adopts a more circumspect approach. He writes that 'although the Ruhr campaign led to a temporary reduction in iron and steel supply it failed to halt the upward direction of German war production, which reached new peaks during 1943'. Krupps lost only 7.6 per cent of its production in 1943, whilst the August-Thyssen plants produced more iron that year than during the previous two. Overall, Overy concludes that 'bombing … only reduced potential German industrial output by around 9 per cent in 1943', which was taken from an economy that from 1941 had expanded its war production considerably, and whilst bombing 'caused local and temporary dislocation', it 'could not prevent German industry from adapting to the pressures and [its] expanding output'.[11]

Overall, it seems safe to conclude that from spring 1943, Bomber Command, now attacking heavily the industrial targets that mattered, caused Germany's war production to gently plateau and thereby forestall a much more dramatic increase in 1944. Ultimately, however, assessing the effects of bombing during the Battle of the Ruhr on Germany's war production and workers' morale was, and remains, extremely difficult.

10   Tooze, A., *The Wages of Destruction: The Making and Breaking of the Nazi War Economy*, Penguin (2007), pp.595–625.

11   Overy, R., *The Bombing War: Europe 1939–1945*, Allen Lane (2013), pp.454–55.

FURTHER READING

The sources available on Bomber Command during World War II are considerable. Cited here are some of the most useful original document files, official accounts, books and articles that provide for further research and additional reading about its strategic bombing campaign against the Ruhr.

Primary sources

The National Archives (TNA) – Kew, London
AIR41/43, Air Ministry and Ministry of Defence: Air Historical Branch: Narratives and Monographs. RAF Narrative (first draft) The RAF in Bomber Offensive against Germany: vol. V The Full Offensive, Feb 1943–Feb 1944

AIR2/8694, Selection of bombing objectives: Air Staff policy, 1940–1944

AIR2/2805, W.A.5 Plan: employment of British Striking Force in attacking Germany's manufacturing resources in the Ruhr in the event of war in 1939, 1937–1940

AIR8/1109, Bombing offensive: effect on German war effort, 1 July 1943–30 June 1944

AIR8/1238, Destruction of German dams: economic effect, 1 Mar 1943–30 Apr 1943

AIR14/2662 & AIR14/2663, Bombers' Baedeker (A Guide to the Economic Importance of German Towns and Cities), Part I (A–K); & Part II (L–Z)

AIR14/3410, Operational Research Section: final reports on operations, night raids, Nos. 280–415 Vol. III, 1 Mar 1943–31 Aug 1943

AIR14/3373 & AIR14/3375, Interception and Tactics: Night Reports, 1 Jan 1943–31 May 1943; & Night Reports, 1 June 1943–31 Dec 1943

AIR14/1204, Dortmund–Ems and Mittelland canals, 1 Sept 1941–28 Feb 1945

AIR14/1199, German anti-aircraft defences, 1 June 1940–30 June 1945

AIR14/1254, Progress of RAF bomber offensive against Germany, 1 Mar 1943–31 Dec 1943

AIR14/1780, MoHS: assessment of bombing damage to German towns, 1 Feb 1943–30 Nov 1945

AIR19/383, Attacks on the Ruhr dams, 1943

AIR19/170, Bombing of German targets: results, 1940–1944

AIR20/300, Air Intelligence paper: Ruhr industries, Germany, 1937–1939

AIR20/280, Western Plan W.A.5(a): the attack of German war industry, 1939–1944

AIR24/253, Bomber Command Quarterly Review, January–February–March 1943, No. 4

AIR24/256, Bomber Command Quarterly Review, April–May–June 1943, No. 5

AIR24/259, Bomber Command Quarterly Review, July–August–September 1943, No. 6

Official Histories, Reports & Memoirs
Air Ministry, *The Rise and Fall of the German Air Force*, The National Archives (2008 ed.)

Bennett, D., *The Pathfinders*, Sphere (1971)

Boog, H., *et. al.*, *Germany and the Second World War, Vol. VII: The Strategic Air War in Europe and the War in the West and East Asia, 1943–1944/5*, OUP (2015 ed.)

British Bombing Survey Unit, *The Strategic Air War Against Germany 1939–1945: The Official Report of the British Bombing Survey Unit*, forewords by MRAF M. Beetham & Maj-Gen J.W. Huston; introduction by S. Cox, Frank Cass (1998)

Greenhous, B., *et. al.*, *The Crucible of War: The Official History of the Royal Canadian Air Force, Volume III*, University of Toronto Press (1994)

Harris, A., *Dispatch on War Operations*, Frank Cass (1995)

Harris, A., *Bomber Offensive*, Pen & Sword (2005 ed.)

Hinsley, F.H., *British Intelligence in the Second World War, vol. III: Its Influence on Strategy and Operations*, HMSO (1984)

Johnen, H., *Duel Under the Stars: The Memoir of a Luftwaffe Night Pilot in World War II*, Foreword by J. Holland, Greenhill (2020 ed.)

Jones, R.V., *Most Secret War: British Scientific Intelligence 1939–1945*, Penguin (2009 ed.)

Thompson, W.R., *Lancaster to Berlin*, Goodall (1997)

Webster, C. & Frankland, N., *The Strategic Air Offensive against Germany 1939–1945, vol. I: Preparation*; *vol. II: Endeavour*; & *vol. IV: Annexes and Appendices*, HMSO (1961)

Books

Friedrich, J., *The Fire: The Bombing of Germany, 1940–1945*, Columbia University Press (2008)

Hastings, M., *Bomber Command*, Pan (2007 ed.)

Middlebrook, M., *Bomber Command War Diaries: An Operational Reference Book, 1939–1945*, Midland (1998)

Murray, W., *Strategy for Defeat: The Luftwaffe 1939–1945*, Air University Press (1983)

Overy, R., *The Bombing War: Europe 1939–1945*, Allen Lane (2013)

Probert, H., *Bomber Harris: His Life and Times*, Greenhill (2006)

Richards, D., *RAF Bomber Command in the Second World War: The Hardest Victory*, Penguin (2001)

Tooze, A., *The Wages of Destruction: The Making and Breaking of the Nazi War Economy*, Penguin (2007)

INDEX